THE LAUGHING PLAYMATE

And Other Stories by Scottish Writers

THE LAUGHING PLAYMATE

and Other Stories
by Scottish Writers
1992

INTRODUCTION BY
Brian McCabe

HarperCollins*Publishers*

HarperCollins*Publishers*
77–85 Fulham Palace Road
Hammersmith, London w6 8jb

First published by HarperCollins*Publishers* 1992
1 3 5 7 9 8 6 4 2

The Publisher acknowledges the financial assistance of the
Scottish Arts Council in the publication of this volume.

A catalogue record for this book
is available from the British Library

ISBN 0 00 224064 5 (hb)
0 00 224054 8 (pb)

Set in Linotron Baskerville by
Rowland Phototypesetting Ltd
Bury St Edmunds, Suffolk

Printed and bound in Great Britain by
Butler & Tanner Ltd, Frome and London

CONTENTS

CONTENTS

INTRODUCTION

Something which has become clear to me from my own struggles with fiction is that the short story is a different beast from the novel. Each makes different demands, both on the writer and the reader. To complicate things, there are many different kinds of short story and that versatility extends to hybrid creatures such as the novella or the prose poem. It was this diversity which was reinforced for me as I read through the submission for the present volume. Some stories left me with a question in my mind about what the short story is, others reinforced the idea that the distinction between the short story and the novel goes deeper than the obvious difference of length. This is clear from the very fact that a novel can sometimes be criticised as 'a long short story' and conversely, a short story can sometimes be damned, and rightly, as a novel in disguise or a chunk of a novel. In the writing of a short story and a novel, there is a difference of approach, because they are essentially different forms.

It is hard to say just what that essential difference is. I could say that the short story is in the nature of a selection of events, characters, moments, encounters, and that the novel tends to be an accumulation of these things – but there are novels and short stories around which would demonstrate that this particular rule can prove the exception to be valid.

Generally I think it is true that the nature of the short story has to do with brevity, economy, selection, intensity of focus. So some of the best short stories suggest a whole world by focussing intensely on a tiny part of it. Some writers make this more emphatic by hanging their story on one central event or object or image.

Something of the art of the short story then, is to do with

leaving things unsaid. By describing one event in detail, the short story writer can imply what has gone before, what will inevitably come after. Thus a relationship can be conjured from a detailed account of one crucial moment in a couple's mutual history. In 'Laughing Woman', by Frank Shon, it is the moment when the man has decided to break it off with the woman. Ultimately, what is convincing and intriguing in this story is the woman's unaccountable reaction – her laughter.

Helen Lamb's 'The Wall' begins: 'Gourlay positioned himself centre-frame in the kitchen doorway where he could not be missed'. Quite a lot has been established in that opening half-sentence. We have a character who is deliberately arranging himself to be noticed – by whom? By the person who is viewing the doorway, the person, if you like, behind the camera, Gourlay's unwilling spectator. As the story unfolds, she becomes, in a sense, the main character – it is she who builds that wall between them. The wall is a symbol, of course, but Helen Lamb makes sure that, first and foremost, it is a real wall, and she takes us through the physical process of its growth with painstaking rigour – we are made to feel the roughness and the weight of those stones used to build it. There is another level of intensity operating here – the writer is using this small encounter to comment on the ways in which men and women relate, or fail to relate, to each other. 'Darkness Made Visible' by Susan Chaney sustains a similar intensity of focus, successfully bringing alive the deep mutual disenchantments of a family by describing an outing in the car. The closing image, of the mother's face reflected in the hub-cap of the car, is both telling and memorable.

Coming from relatively 'new' writers, these stories are remarkably assured demonstrations of what the short story can achieve in a very few pages.

There are of course stories from more established writers included in the present volume. All stories are submitted to the editors without the names of the authors, yet I've heard people say that it must be easy to recognise the work of well-known writers. What they tend to forget is that the process of encountering the work of many different writers militates against such instant recognition, so that even a writer who has carved out his own fictional territory and has established a distinctive way of writing can easily remain anonymous in the minds of the editors. The nearest I came to 'spotting-the-author' was with the story 'Wonderful Land', which I took to be the work of a writer who had more or less decided to stake a claim on Alan Spence's fictional territory. I thought it a very real and moving story, and vaguely wondered how Alan Spence would feel about his new rival. That is surely a comment on Alan Spence's ability to mine a vein of experience he has written about before and yet remain fresh. Similarly, none of us suspected for a moment that 'In the German Hospital' was by Iain Crichton Smith, though we acknowledged the strength and power of the story. There is no greater vindication of his ability – the story itself is the thing, not the fact that it is one of his.

The Laughing Playmate is the twentieth volume of Scottish Short Stories. The fact that it has sustained itself for so long, continues to be an important outlet for short story writers and is selling better than ever, can only attest to its validity. Let's hope it continues.

BRIAN McCABE

ix

THE LAUGHING PLAYMATE
Kevin Laing

I met Raymond on the third last day, when I was sick to death of Hancock's Holiday Camp. Sick to death of the penny arcades, the rows of brightly-coloured holiday-maker chalets, the candyfloss, the toffee-apples, the childish children's competitions, the stink of beer on my dad's breath when he came home at night. Sick to death of the always-crowded outdoor swimming pool and the wasp-infested beach, which was also a feature of the Hancock's Holiday Camp enclosure.

On the beach I discovered that the stench of sun-tan lotion and the yelling of all the kids gave me headaches. I gathered that my mum was worried about me. I overheard her talking with my dad.

'He has headaches all the time. I think he needs glasses.'

'It's just the sun. Don't worry so much about him.'

'I can't help it. He gets so moody. He's so quiet, and he hasn't made any friends here.'

'All kids go through phases like that. It's normal. He's growing up.'

'But what's the matter with him? He wanders around like a ghost. It's like he's in another world.'

'There's nothing the matter with him. It's a phase.'

'Don't you care about him?'

'Let's not go through all that again.'

'Maybe if you spent more time with him . . . Wasn't that why we came here?'

I didn't linger to hear the rest of the conversation, because I knew they were going to start picking on each other again.

I met Raymond when I was sitting on a plastic bench near the Laughing Playmate.

The Laughing Playmate sat inside a glass case in the middle of Hancock Palace, a large enclosed area with a glass roof containing stalls, arcades, a pub, a souvenir shop, and other places designed to encourage holiday-makers to part with their money.

You put a coin in a slot and the Laughing Playmate, sitting on his tall, narrow platform, started to laugh. He rolled on the ball-like base which he had instead of legs, and tinny laughter poured out of him. This laughter sounded as if it came from a large transistor radio turned up to full volume inside his fat belly.

His fibreglass body was painted with the uniform of the Hancock's Holiday Camp Playmates, that army of sunnily-smiling young people who got paid for going around returning lost infants to their owners and generally making sure everyone was having a fun time.

On my first day at the camp, when I had drifted away from my parents to find out what the place had to offer for a shy twelve-year-old hard-to-please loner like myself, I had put a coin in the slot as a matter of course. The sound of that laughter and the sight of that milkshake-pink balloon-sized face with its fixed grin had made me feel depressed. It was the same as the feeling I usually got when I heard my parents picking on each other.

I decided that I wouldn't be putting any more coins into that particular slot. I would save my money for better things.

But time after time I would watch other kids putting money in and giggling and nudging each other as if they were doing something naughty.

How could they find the Laughing Playmate funny? Couldn't they hear that it was not really laughter?

I was sitting on the bench, wearing my Hancock's shorts and the green plastic sunglasses that my mum had bought me in the belief that it would put a stop to my headaches. The place was quite empty, and I supposed that everybody had swarmed down to the beach to lie in the sun.

Suddenly the Laughing Playmate burst into life, rollicking and roaring with laughter, his eyes creased with the effort. I jumped up in alarm, because I hadn't seen anybody putting money in the slot. I took off the sunglasses, thinking that maybe they had blinded me. I felt as if the Laughing Playmate was laughing at my shocked, blinking expression.

Then I saw the pale face of a skinny boy of about my age staring at me from the other side of the glass case. I wanted to run away and hide my embarrassment, but something about the boy's face made me stay. It was a face that was neither happy nor sad. It was simply watchful.

The boy came round to where I was standing. 'Funny, isn't he?'

He had a flat voice. He waited a long time for me to answer. He gazed directly at me, as if his cool blue eyes wanted to prise into my head.

Since arriving at the camp I hadn't felt like speaking to anyone my own age. But under the brutal intimacy of this boy's gaze I felt myself weakening. I had a sudden urge to release the tightness in my stomach and blabber out all the feelings and thoughts that had been brewing up inside me during the last week and a half. His silence was like an invitation for me to do just this.

But I said nothing. The boy glanced at the Laughing Playmate.

'Of course, he's not all that he seems, you know.'

I pondered for a moment on this puzzling adult expression.

'What do you mean?'

'You should come here after midnight. Then you'd see what I mean.'

Surely he was pulling my leg, but there was no teasing gleam in his eyes. I tried to return his gaze, but my eyes began to water and I looked away.

The Laughing Playmate stopped abruptly, his body tilted to one side. I thought this odd, since he normally went on for much longer and grew quieter towards the end, as if pulling himself together. It sounded like the laughter had got stuck in his throat. The boy didn't seem to notice anything strange in this. He was clearly thinking of deeper things. I felt his eyes boring into my head.

3

'You look as if you're having a rotten time,' he said at last. 'What's up? Got another headache, have you?'

I stared at him through the water in my eyes.

'Your mum and dad been getting on each other's nerves again?'

I blushed. My mind raced to keep up with my emotions. Who was he? How did he know these things about me? He must be playing some nasty trick, I thought, and I was too slow-witted to understand. Yet his voice was still flat.

'They pick on each other a lot, don't they?'

I moved to put on the plastic sunglasses again, but he pulled them out of my fingers with a curiously gentle movement.

'My name's Raymond,' he said. 'What's yours?'

I snatched back the sunglasses and hid my face.

'That's none of your business.' My voice was squeaky. I walked towards the main doorway on wobbly legs, afraid that he might grab my arm and tell me more intimate secrets about myself. I turned to get one last look at him. He had disappeared.

I watched a small girl in pigtails put a coin in the Laughing Playmate's slot, and saw a peevish look spreading over her face.

'Mummy! Mummy! It doesn't work.'

Anxiety followed me around for the rest of the day. The brief meeting loomed in my mind like a memory of a humiliation. How could he know those things? Why did he have to stare right into me like that? He must be spying on me, shadowing me, finding out more about me. I felt exposed.

And how come I hadn't seen him already during the time I had been roaming around in the enclosure?

I sat for a long time on one of the deck chairs for spectators beside the swimming pool, hiding my dread behind the sunglasses. Was he still out there somewhere spying on me? There was no sign of him among the rushing, diving, splashing kids.

That evening my dad went off to the Eldorado, the smoky pub at the far end of Hancock Palace where he spent a lot of his time. With an air of martyrdom my mum took me to see a variety show.

Anxiety stayed with me. As I sat in the audience I kept looking round, feeling sure that I would soon see the boy's eyes singling me out.

Under normal circumstances the variety show would have delighted me. I had seen some of the performers before on TV. There was a singer, some comedians, a conjurer, and dancers.

Then what was announced as a troupe of Italian acrobats, of different ages and sizes, all with slicked-back hair and tight waistcoats, skipped onto the stage and began leaping around on seesaws and making human pyramids.

Suddenly the whole whirling spectacle seemed to freeze for a moment as I stared. One of the younger acrobats looked familiar. Was it the boy who had spoken to me, his hair now dyed black and plastered with grease? I strained forward in my seat, half expecting him to turn and look at me. But I was being an idiot. What had got into me? The boy in Hancock Palace hadn't spoken with an Italian accent. Besides, this boy on the stage wasn't so skinny.

But there was something odd about him, anyway. Unlike the others he wasn't doing any acrobatics. He was just walking about, observing the others, as if pretending to supervise, his face blank.

A little later one of the comedians caught my attention, and I forgot my anxiety for a while. He had a square, sweating face, and he tried to juggle with three balls, but he was clumsy and kept dropping them. He was dumbfounded, because sometimes the balls bounced, but sometimes they just plonked down like lumps of plasticine.

I laughed aloud, and turned to look at my mum. She was sitting with a stony expression, seeing neither me nor the comedian. I was learning to live with these odd adult expressions, just as I was learning to live with headaches, but they saddened me. I stopped laughing. The comedian and his stupid plasticine balls now seemed idiotic, and I turned my attention back to the audience. Surely there was a pair of cool blue eyes somewhere taking note of me and my mum.

The next morning, the second last day at the camp, I lifted the bag of pocket money that was always left for me on the kitchen table, and went out of the chalet into the July sunshine.

Normally, having nothing better to do, I would head straight for Hancock Palace to kill some time on the penny arcades. But on this day the thought of meeting the boy again stopped me.

I wandered aimlessly, frustrated at having my morning routine disturbed. Twice I watched the cable car clanking over the enclosure above my head and disappearing over the chalet roofs.

In my mind's eye I saw the boy's face. I couldn't picture it clearly, and it struck me that it was like trying to remember the face of a shop-window dummy.

I thought about his voice, trying to recall any subtle hints of irony or aggression. But no, the voice had been as blank as the face.

I remembered the gentle way he had taken my sunglasses. His hand, when it touched mine briefly, had been cool and limp. How could such a touch inspire fear?

I thought about the way he had gazed directly at me, and how my eyes had watered. I must have looked like a sickly baby. It irritated me that I couldn't remember the mood in the boy's eyes. Had there been sympathy there when he spoke of my headaches and my parents? Or a secretly mocking glint?

What was his name? Raymond. The name itself, neither common nor obscure, seemed somehow ambiguous. He had wanted to know my name, and like a scared rabbit I had run away.

At last, after I had weighed up all my impressions, my anxiety dispersed. He wasn't a threat to me, I decided. I made my way to Hancock Palace, sat down in front of the Laughing Playmate, and waited.

After a few minutes the fat fibreglass figure began to laugh and roll on its platform. I stood up and took off the sunglasses. Raymond was looking at me through the glass case. I walked round and stood beside him. I put the sunglasses in my pocket and told him my name.

I realised that, once again, I hadn't seen anybody putting money in the slot. But now, having accepted Raymond, it seemed easy to accept the mystery.

I wondered if I was boring him with my questions, but I couldn't stop. He was laconic, and didn't appear particularly interested in me today.

'How long have you been here?'

'Ages.'

'Are you here with your mum and dad?'

'My mum and dad have split up.'

'How come you're here then?'

'Nowhere else to go.'

We walked in a circle, past the stalls and shops. He paused to study a thin old lady sitting on a bench scribbling postcards.

'But what do you do here?'

'I watch people. Don't you? What else is there to do?'

He was going to be dull company, I thought.

'There's lots to do.'

'Is there?'

'Well, there's the penny arcades, the beach, the competitions . . . There's the . . .'

His blank stare silenced me, and he began to walk away.

'Wait! What did you mean yesterday when you said that about the Laughing Playmate?'

He turned and looked at me closely, as if making sure of something. I was pleased to be the centre of his attention again.

'It's true,' he said. 'He's not all that he seems.'

'You mean you come here at night and watch him?'

'That's the best time to watch people.'

'But what does he do at night?'

I braced myself, waiting for a sarcastic grin to contort the numb-looking features of his face. But his expression was changeless. 'Come tonight and see,' he said.

He left me, and vanished through a side-exit. I had a picture of him entering some night-time world, different from this day-time reality which clearly bored him. It seemed impossible that he could look so sombre all the time. I wanted to follow him, wherever he was going. I felt that we were one of a kind.

Through the chink in the door I could see my mum reading, or pretending to read, in the tiny lamplit living room. By the look on her face I guessed that she had gone into a huff again. My dad had gone out drinking. I drifted into shallow sleep, from which I was awoken by bedsprings creaking in the room next door. The living room was now in darkness, and I guessed that my dad had come back. They would be whisper-ing so as not to wake me.

I slept again. The next thing I knew I was sitting up in bed, wide awake, as if some dream-land alarm clock had just gone off.

I tiptoed to the kitchen and saw on the luminous dial of the clock that it was after one. The idea of joining Raymond on his vigil excited me, yet it seemed impossible and forbidden. I sat brooding on my bed for a long time.

Soon I would be leaving Hancock's Holiday Camp, I reasoned. Surely I could allow myself an adventure, after so much boredom.

I pulled on my clothes and padded out into Hancock's night-world.

I nearly didn't make it to Hancock Palace. There were lamps along the pathways, but the darkness between them and behind the hedges tempted me to run back to bed. I thought of a terrifying werewolf film I had recently been allowed to see. I felt that I had just stepped into it. I thought of the story of Tam O'Shanter being chased by witches that I had learned at school. Now it didn't seem so comical. What if a witch flew out and clutched my ankles?

I hadn't expected to see anybody on the way, but I was

wrong. Passing the outdoor swimming pool I noticed someone sitting on a deck chair on the opposite side. I saw that it was the chair where I had sat after my first meeting with Raymond. The figure was a boy of about my age, looking ghostly in the lamplight. At first I thought it might be Raymond, but his face was the wrong shape. The expression on his face, though, was the same serious one that Raymond wore. I realised that he was gazing at me intently. He was not a frightening figure, but I hurried away.

I passed the hall where the variety show had been held. I stopped and peeped in through a low window, wondering if this was one of the places where Raymond watched people. I noticed a dim light inside. A small area of the stage was lit up, and I saw someone sitting on one end of a seesaw. I recognised him at once as the Italian boy whom I had mistaken for Raymond during the show. His waistcoat was unbuttoned, his greased hair was unsticking itself, and he appeared to be waiting for someone to join him on the other end of the seesaw. I moved on quickly when I saw that this boy, who also wore Raymond's expression, was gazing in my direction. Neither of the boys, I realised, looked surprised to see me.

At the main entrance to Hancock Hall I saw another boy. He was standing beside a drinking-fountain with his hands in his pockets, as if keeping guard. I nodded to him, but he didn't move. I found myself frowning. I felt like walking over and shaking him. Why were they all so passive?

No doubt Raymond would explain about the boys, I thought. Perhaps they were his friends.

The main doorway had glass panels in it, through which I could see a faint light. When I stepped inside I saw that the light shone from a bulb right above the Laughing Playmate's head. The next thing I noticed was the muffled sound of music and voices from the Eldorado pub at the far end, which I had expected to be closed. Then I glimpsed a boy emerging from the shadows of a strangely silent penny-arcade and vanishing through a side-exit. The serious look on his face, now so familiar, irritated me. Did they all look the same?

9

I sat down on the bench where I had twice already met Raymond, feeling sure that he would make the same magical sort of appearance. I avoided looking at the Laughing Playmate, because in the ghostly light his mute pinkish-grey face seemed sinister.

I sat for a long time, and began to feel disappointed in this would-be adventure. I felt that Raymond was letting me down, even though we had made no definite agreement to meet. This night-time world, populated by solemn boys, was beginning to seem pretty dull.

Suddenly a picture came into my head of myself sitting there on the bench. I must look just like the other boys, I thought. Like them I was waiting, watching. Did I have that same expression on my face?

For no apparent reason I remembered words my mum had spoken.

'He's so quiet . . . He wanders around like a ghost. It's like he's in another world.'

I was on the point of sneaking back to the chalet when the door of the Eldorado pub flew open behind me. Noises from inside became distinct for a few seconds before the door swung back. I scurried to find a hiding-place in the nearest penny-arcade, and crouched in the shadows. I didn't want to be spotted by an adult. How would I be able to explain myself?

A drunk man staggered from the pub, his feet shuffling on the tiled floor, his head bowed forward. He was wearing loose summer clothes, and had sandals on his sockless feet. It was his feet that I recognised first. It was my dad.

My childish heart sank into desolation at the sight of my dad in the guise of a drunk. Was Raymond watching? Night-time, he had said, was the best time for watching people.

My dad went up to the Laughing Playmate's glass case, fumbled in his pockets, and put a coin in the slot. 'Bloody thing doesn't work.'

He twisted round, and for a moment I thought he was going to stagger back to the pub and complain. But he turned and kicked the aluminium strip at the base of the case and thumped his fist on the glass.

The Laughing Playmate reacted. It rolled and chuckled, but the sound coming from its transistorised innards sounded even less like laughter than usual. It was the sound of something in pain. A choked trapped-animal sound.

My dad leaned forward, closed his eyes, and pressed his forehead against the glass.

The sobbing and choking grew louder, and the body of the dummy rocked faster. It looked as if it was struggling to extricate itself from a pool of glue. My dad didn't move.

The sobbing became an angry growling, and the rocking grew furious, the fat figure's face set in grim grey determination. It seemed to be making a tremendous effort to break loose. I was sure that the glass case was trembling, and that my dad must be feeling the vibrations against his forehead. But still he didn't move.

I noticed a boy nearby in the shadows watching him.

As I crouched, hypnotised by this madness, a queer thought struck me. Was this not the Laughing Playmate's usual performance? Were the echoes and the lighting in this night-time Hancock Palace making everything look and sound different? Was this madness only in my imagination?

The Laughing Playmate was now roaring so loudly that I wondered why nobody came running from the pub. Its body swung so much that I feared its head would shatter the side of the case. Still my dad stood motionless, like someone sleeping on his feet, heedless of the danger.

At last, after what felt to me like a long nightmare, the dummy sat silent, like a monstrous child after a tantrum. Looking sad and exhausted, my dad stood up straight and sighed.

I had an urge to run and hug him, and make him tell me that everything was all right. I wanted him to carry me back to the chalet, put me to bed, kiss me, and tell me again that everything was all right. He must wake up mum so that she could kiss me too, tuck me up like a little child, and tell me again that really, really, everything was all right.

But I couldn't move.

As my dad disappeared through the doorway a hand landed

on my shoulder. I turned in panic and hit out with my arm into the darkness. I saw that it was Raymond, and that I had just struck the side of his head. He straightened himself up, his face wan in the dim light. His gaze was calm, and his hand stayed on my shoulder.

'You see? It's just like I said. He's not all that he seems. But you knew that already, didn't you?'

I looked towards the Laughing Playmate, and saw that another boy was now sitting on the bench, his face a sober mask. All the boys were wearing that same mask. Raymond was just one of many.

'So now you've joined us,' he said. 'There's quite a few of us around here.'

I batted his hand away from my shoulder and sprang to my feet. Two other boys had emerged from the shadows, both of them watching me.

'What are you talking about? I haven't joined anybody. Who are you, anyway? What's the matter with you? And what's the matter with *them*?'

'We're all right. There's nothing the matter with any of us.'

'Yes, there is. There must be. You're mad. You're all going about here like ghosts. Why don't you *do* something?'

'We are doing something.'

'What?'

'Watching people.'

'No, I mean . . . Why don't you . . .'

Now I was almost shouting. My voice was quavering, but I didn't care. I thought about the adults in the pub who might be able to hear me, but I didn't care.

'Why don't you play? Why don't you talk to each other? Why don't you pull my leg and make fun of me? I wouldn't mind. Really, I wouldn't. Why don't you laugh? Or cry? Or shout? Why don't you *do* something?'

I was surrounded by boys, all as silent as fish. My hands shook with a desire to hit one of them. I dashed over to the Laughing Playmate, kicked the aluminium strip, and thumped on the glass.

'*Do* something!'

Tears leapt down my cheeks as the dummy exploded into life. The numb faces of the boys looked on.

'Don't look at me like that!'

I closed my eyes, pressed my forehead hard against the glass, and prayed that they would disappear. The Laughing Playmate laughed and cried and rolled and choked and chuckled and sobbed and cackled and howled and roared . . .

In my mind I was inside the glass case, and the convulsions were coming from my own belly. Everything that had been bottled up inside there was being released. I laughed and cried and howled and chuckled and . . . It took a long time, for there was a lot to come out.

When it was all over I looked round and saw that all the boys had vanished. I was exhausted, and it felt as if many hours had passed. I left Hancock Palace and looked up at the stars. The night sky seemed as beautiful and vast as my relief. I met no one on my way back to the chalet. By the time I stepped into the dark living room I had forgotten that the boys had ever existed. I closed the door noisily behind me. The light snapped on in my mum and dad's bedroom.

'It's all right,' I said. 'I'm back.'

Groggy with sleep, they stumbled out to greet me.

THE LIGHTS OF AMERICA
Donald Munro

'Straight to bed!' shouted Mum after us from the living room. 'And no story!'

'He's over-tired,' she said to Granny, 'it's the change of air.'

For myself, I felt just the same in Lewis as in Glasgow, but I knew that on the island I could run about like crazy, shout indoors, leave my dinner but eat my pudding, and stay up late – all thanks to the change of air.

Grandad took my hand and led me to the half-landing. He stopped there and pulled back the net curtain from the window. A vase of plastic flowers – 'A Present From Wick' – fell over. He paused with his finger to his lips. I giggled behind my hand. The window was small and set deep in the wall. The narrow frame had been painted with a broad brush and the glass was still smeared red. He put out the hall light and we stood together at the window.

'What can you see out there, *a'bhalaich*?'

There was only darkness. Two darknesses – the low sky, mottled with clouds, and the Atlantic, huge and restless, splashed with white. The sun had gone completely.

'Nothing,' I whispered back.

'Och now. A fine sailor you'd make. Can you not see a light?'

I strained in all directions until, suddenly, far to the right, a beam of white cut across the sea.

'The lighthouse!' I said aloud. I shooshed myself. 'You can see the lighthouse from here.'

'Well, yes, the lighthouse. But that's not what I mean. Can you not see a light – out there?'

He pointed into the enormous blackness. I peered after him, guessing at the horizon. But I could see nothing.

'Do you know,' he took his time over every word, 'that if you look long enough and hard enough you can see the lights of America?'

'New York!'

'Yes, very likely New York.'

I stared and stared. Nothing.

'Do you not need a telescope, Grandad?'

'Och no,' he laughed quietly. 'The air is very clear up here.'

'Can *you* see them, Grandad?'

'My eyesight's not what it was, *a'bhalaich*. But they're out there. I saw them often enough as a boy myself. You stand there and you'll see them. It's a secret, though. Just between yourself and myself.'

He left me there and went back into the living room. As he closed the door behind him he said, 'Wheesht!' Not to me, but to the others. I stared into the night.

I awoke in bed in the morning. I didn't remember going. Grandad had finished breakfast by the time I got downstairs. He was in the byre sharpening tools, said Granny. I could go and see him if I stood well back.

'Well hello, lazy!' he called as I went in. 'You slept the clock round last night!'

'I didn't see them, Grandad.' I hung my head. 'I fell asleep.'

'Oh dear!' he said seriously. 'Never mind. Maybe you'll see them tonight.'

'I hope so. Have you ever been to America, Grandad? Have you seen New York?'

'Never.' I was disappointed and maybe it showed. He said, 'I was in New Zealand and Australia.'

'Did you see a kangaroo?' I asked with new interest. We had done Australia at school.

'Thousands.' And we talked of kangaroos and dingos until lunchtime.

All that summer, and for summers afterwards, I looked for the lights of America. I wanted to see New York. Once I did see a light, small and pale. I told Grandad and he said, yes, that was it. But I wasn't to tell anyone – it was still a secret.

Back in Glasgow I told my teacher. She laughed. Then, to

my horror, she told the secret to the whole class. They all laughed too and she said, 'Can anyone tell me why David could not have seen the lights of America?' and turned the whole thing in to a geography lesson.

At my desk I fought with tears. At playtime I fought with the other boys who jeered at me without mercy. They didn't know Lewis. They didn't understand anything about it. After Ness there was nothing until America and I had seen it. So had Grandad. I didn't look again, though. I had shared my secret and the magic had gone.

It struck me that this is the first time I have visited Lewis in winter. As a child I had called myself a Leodhasach. Leodhasach, Siarach, Niseach: I lapped the words with my tongue to baffled friends and teachers. But this is my first winter.

We were met at the plane by two cousins. At first the conversation was bland and comfortless. Yes, he was a good man. He would be badly missed. Seonaid was taking it as well as could be expected. We are poor comforters; only He can comfort her now. After some miles my grandfather's death had been talked over completely. The illness had given us time, I suppose, to prepare ourselves. As the Atlantic appeared on the horizon of the Barvas road, my mother turned to me and said, melodramatically, 'I feel we're really home now.'

I thought of the same scene in a luxury car commercial where the businessman finds freedom from executive stress on this very road, miraculously close to the city.

'Oh yes,' said one of the cousins, 'you're all at home here. Would you not like to live here better than Glasgow, David?'

They asked me the same question every summer as a child. I always said yes. This time I thought he was really asking.

'There's no work,' I said.

'No. No there isn't. That's very true.'

He turned then to my mother and his voice relaxed in Gaelic. 'It is a year now since you were home, Murdina.'

'Yes and nearly two,' and she drew in her breath as she said it, just as my father used to, when imitating her accent.

'You didn't lose your Gaelic then?'

'Where would I lose it? In a puddle?'

They laughed, weakly: the first smile of the journey. Even I laughed, having half caught the joke. My mother didn't make them often. I knew, then, that she had been annoyed.

The house was almost unrecognisable. Everything was as before but it was barren of comfort and seemed like a stranger's home. All the cheap china and glass, the plastic stag's-head barometer, the aerial photo of the croft, now looked to me like any other house in Ness. Whatever had made it my home had gone, or was lost in the chill of sorrow.

My mother and grandmother broke down in each other's arms. My grandmother wailed aloud and even through my own tears I turned away in discomfort, almost in distaste. The trestles – well worn – stood in the centre of the floor, on the patterned rug that had been for me a car park and a battle-field. I was virtually unmoved by the open coffin and the thick, pale face. My mother said, 'He looks so like himself!' and stopped sobbing. I barely knew him.

The arrangements for the next day's funeral were gone over in Gaelic. I struggled to make out the words – and struggled more to make sense of them. Now and then one of the men would turn to me and make a point clear in English. My mother said, 'He understands every word you say,' just as she did of the dog. So I followed as best I could and got most of it. 'Lifting the books. Taking a lift. Taking a cord.'

My mother told me twice that whatever might be said at the graveside by the minister it would not be a prayer.

'What will it be, then?' I asked.

'Just words,' she said, exasperated. 'For God's sake don't thank him for the prayer!'

I laughed out loud, then withered in shame as they all turned to look at me, without anger, just in empty surprise.

We had been over the funeral again and again. No doubt they were concerned that I, so close and yet so much an outsider, might do something wrong. Again and again I had been told of the dignity and simplicity.

There were prayers that night: prayers long and desolate and uncomfortably beautiful as the road home over the moor.

Prayers in voices cracked and unsure, ill made for speaking aloud yet well used to praying. Prayers I strained to understand from a life and death so alien that I doubted I had any part in it. I was peering into a world as dark and hidden from me as the Atlantic night.

After a while sitting with the open casket I almost forgot that Grandad was there too. I had been looking out of the corner of my eye at the dumb grey screen of the TV. I had missed *thirtysomething* – I never usually missed it.

I said how tired I was from the journey, that I would go up to bed.

'Yes, you must be,' said Granny. 'It's the change of air.'

At the half-landing the vase from Wick was still behind the curtain. The window-frame had been painted green – the glass now smeared green and red. I wasn't surprised to see a light on the horizon: a tanker going up north, no doubt. There was a red light blinking in the sky: a jet, heading for America, where it would catch the sun that had set on this island already. I remembered clearly the aching shame of the teacher's laughter.

In bed, I went over the funeral arrangements in my own mind. I tried to imagine how I would look in my father's greatcoat. I wept a little for Grandad, or for myself. At last I went down to sleep, wondering what I had missed on *thirtysomething*.

THE FANTASY DOOR
Alison Armstrong

Lock the fantasy door and keep it shut. That seemed the only way to survive Aunt Crabtree's School for Wayward Girls. Within days of my arrival, I was caught daydreaming in sewing class, and was put into Solitary for this crime. The School for Wayward Girls taught Virtue, Industry and Morality, and Facing Up To Reality was an important part of these three subjects.

Solitary was a locked room in the cellar, which was baking hot, even in winter. You weren't allowed to remove your clothes – that was indecent – so you cooked. You were completely cooked up. The heat and the solitude brought to life whatever dross was in your mind, and the inhabitants of your subconscious gave you hell. I was plagued by goblins who feasted on my head, my heart and my privates, and from time to time belched morsels of my chewed-up flesh. Lock the Fantasy Door. If I hadn't done so, I would have turned into a fruitcake.

The School for Wayward Girls let you choose your own destruction. You could escape through your imagination – and have your imagination tear you apart in the cellar. Or, playing safe, you could wall yourself up inside reality. Reality was the school: peeling wallpaper, constant sewing, and being told you were worth nothing.

Reality had turned my fellow students into dumb girls who'd left fear and panic behind. I called them Gingerbread Girls because their faces looked flat and because they were thoroughly baked and ready to be eaten. They were successful students; no longer wayward, but passive, uncomplaining and useless. They stared at me all the time, making my soul feel like frayed rope. What they did on Saturday nights frightened me.

On Saturday nights, the girls would sit on their beds and cut themselves with bits of broken glass they'd managed to sneak past Aunt Crabtree. If the libido didn't flow, blood did, but the girls' faces showed no sign of pain or relief. I wasn't tempted to join the bloodletting rituals: not only was I squeamish, but I had to stay apart from the other girls. They showed me what I'd become if I wasn't careful, and I had to take care because I wanted to be an architect like my father. He knew I had potential; otherwise he wouldn't have given me the serious, undemonstrative support I'd known for years. In that time we'd become close – perhaps closer than father and daughter ought to be, but our relationship had stayed intellectual. Approval *had been* my father's way of showing love. But it had all turned to nothing, as I was wasted at Aunt Crabtree's.

Her regime brought self-extinction; a gift if you'd done something you wanted to forget, like murder. I'd done nothing I was ashamed of. I'd burned down Natasha's boutique, but I'd made sure that nobody was inside – and the burning served Natasha right. She was the female dog of model-girl proportions who'd taken away my father.

Natasha was sly. She knew my father and I were close, so she couldn't storm around and demand revenge. 'Debbie needs special help,' she'd purred to my father and the next thing I knew, I was packed off to Aunt Crabtree's for the school's unique form of therapy.

Only it wasn't therapy. It was neutering.

I wasn't mad when they sent me there. I repeated my name – Deborah Blackwood – during the endless sewing classes, to hold on to something that made sense, amid Aunt Crabtree's crazily outmoded ideas about education. If only there'd been matches in the school ... If the Gingerbread Girls had smuggled broken glass, surely I could have smuggled matches. I didn't try, because I knew that torching the place would solve nothing. The School for Wayward Girls wasn't just bricks and mortar. It was an idea. People wanted the school because the enforcement of Victorian virtues made them feel safe. Letters of commendation from the Education Minister hung on the school walls, concealing stains and peeling paper. The government was happy that Aunt Crabtree was Doing Something about juvenile delinquency, and that made people happy. I wasn't happy, but then, I counted for nothing.

Being a dutiful couple, my father and Natasha came to visit me one day. I was taken out of sewing class and, still clutching the shirt I was making, I was escorted to the Visiting Room.

Aunt Crabtree personally supervised the Visiting Room. She stood, or patrolled; a mountain of flesh turned into granite. The cerise suit she wore beneath her graduation gown suited neither her figure nor her personality. It was too frivolous. Perhaps she was wearing it because there were men in the room, I thought irreverently. This was the first time I'd seen Aunt Crabtree among other adults and her authority was slightly less overwhelming than usual.

There were various friends and loved ones dotted about the room, trying to make contact with Gingerbread Girls. Their failure to do so should have been a warning to my father, but he wasn't taking any notice. He was too busy gazing at Natasha.

'Excuse me,' I said pointedly. Father put on an expression of gloom, which suited his reserved bearing.

'My daughter. My daughter,' he muttered as he held me close. Beneath the gloom, he was *glowing*. It was Natasha's influence. As long as he continued glowing, there was no chance of me going home.

'Get me out of here,' I said, to see what effect this would have.

Natasha smiled sweetly. 'We can't, darling,' she said. 'You've been certified.'

Nasty conniving bitch. I counted to ten slowly and looked around the room. The Gingerbread Girls were showing no recognition of their visitors – and if their guests were like Natasha I didn't blame them. 'I'm more sane than anyone here,' I snapped. Let Aunt Crabtree hear me: I was only saying what she knew.

Natasha had followed my gaze, to humour me. 'Catatonic,' she observed, glancing at the Gingerbread Girls. She'd been reading! She had nothing else to do, now that Modes Uniques was a blackened shell.

I contradicted her. 'No. Gingerbread Girls.'

The impact this had was startling. Natasha put on an attentive expression – slight frown, alert posture – to show she was taking me seriously. 'Gingerbread Girls,' she repeated, trying to sound intellectual. No doubt she was attempting to impress my father. He had more understanding in his little finger than she had in her immaculate head. *He* had the intelligence to remain silent when he couldn't say anything worthwhile. Not that he needed to speak – he knew what I was driving at. I had the old fairy story in mind: the one with the witch and the candy house . . . and the wicked stepmother. I wondered if he was disturbed by the comparison, or whether, in his usual silent manner, he was enjoying my ingenuity.

I explained myself for Natasha's benefit. 'This place fries your brains until –' I said this euphemism loudly for Aunt Crabtree's benefit – 'you're totally *cooked*. Look at them. They can't do anything except stare into space and wait to be eaten up.' Then I held up the shirt I was making. 'This is what I do.'

The shirt was awful. It was in a rough material, with stripes I hadn't matched at the seams. Both sleeves were too long, and one was much longer than the other. 'I'm learning to sew,' I explained.

This struck me as funny, and I heard my ill-modulated laughter dominate the room. Normally inscrutable, my father looked almost guilty, but Natasha kept her sweet composure. 'When you get better, you can sew for my new boutique,' she said as if she were granting me, the basket-case, an unheard-of opportunity.

'I'm not working for an artificial bitch like you,' I shouted. Aunt Crabtree came thundering over, to be restrained by a raised hand and a smile from Natasha the Peacemaker.

I was worried. Did the laughter, followed by the outburst, mean that I was losing my marbles? If so, I wasn't losing them in the way Aunt Crabtree wanted, and she was bound to put me in the cellar.

'I'm sorry,' I said, looking at my father. I felt guilty for being like him and being considered mad. He set light to problems, too: imperfect drawings and models went up in flames, and I'd heard him talk of pouring petrol over people he didn't like. Usually, his civilised reserve concealed his temper, but somebody he worked with had found out. Mad Blackwood, they called him at work, and I knew the nickname frightened him. He was afraid that one day he'd go too far. The glow that Natasha had given him allowed him to hide his fear – which was probably why he liked her. When he looked at her, he saw sweet reason; when he looked at me, he saw himself.

I felt excluded, dead to them.

In the background, Aunt Crabtree was hovering. She had the looks I destined for Natasha: piggy eyes, puffy jowls and clump of receding, overpermed hair. What would my father do on the day he woke up to *that*?

'I know it's difficult, but if you could bring your visit to a close now . . .' Aunt Crabtree was smarmy because she was dealing with paying adults. She was giving my father an extra-special understanding look, that didn't suit the face of an old boar. Her lips had been painted cerise to match her suit, but most of the colour had worn off. She'd been licking her chops in expectation of what she was going to do to me.

My father didn't play her game, but responded to her look with a blank, hostile stare. Even though I knew my father disliked hypocrisy (unless it came from Natasha), I was surprised by the extent of his hatred. I was pleased too – did it mean I would be going home?

Natasha, of course, made the expected response. 'We're just about to leave,' she said, standing up and straightening her skirt. She bent down to kiss me. 'Bye bye, darling.'

My father said nothing. There was nothing within integrity that he could have said, so I was glad he kept quiet. In an absentminded way, he pocketed the shirt I'd been sewing. It was a poor substitute for me.

I watched them leave the room. They made an odd couple; Natasha, the dream of every man, all legs and perfume. Beside her, my father looked stunted, and my shirt, bulging out of his coat pocket, distorted his outline and made him look pathetic . . .

Aunt Crabtree followed them out, doubtless to assure them that my outburst would not go unpunished. When she reappeared, she was angry. She dragged me out of the room, holding my arm in a pincer-like grip. 'You are a foul-mouthed, disrespectful little slut,' she told me.

This was good news, as it confirmed I wasn't a Gingerbread Girl – yet. 'It's true – what I said about Natasha,' I protested. Answering back couldn't make things worse than they already were. I was going to hell – and I was better going there as a maniac than as a compliant lump. Aunt Crabtree wanted lumps to come out of her cellar. Not maniacs.

'What did you *say?*' asked Aunt Crabtree, dangerously. (Talk like a bad girl, Debbie, I like it. But you won't be doing it for long.)

'I said she was an artificial bitch.' I spoke quickly, because this was my death sentence and I wanted to get it over. I could have bought time by mumbling and pretending not to remember, but what was the point? I was going below, whatever I said. Natasha wanted it, so it was inevitable.

I followed Aunt Crabtree along the school corridors, and down the steps into hell. I was meek – a different person from the girl who'd fired Natasha's boutique. Aunt Crabtree's had had *some* effect, even if I'd only learned hopelessness. There was so much madness flying around that I didn't want to add to it by screaming and crying. The school was founded on insanity because it locked up normal people like me.

We came to the Solitary cell. Aunt Crabtree unlocked the door and peered inside. In the dusk, I could see another person, huddled in the far corner. Aunt Crabtree acknowledged this person with a sniff and a 'Hmph', then shoved me inside.

I was now on the wrong side – or was it the right side? – of the Fantasy Door, and I had somebody to share my dreams.

24

It had to be one of the Gingerbread Girls and I didn't relish being pursued into oblivion by her vacant, staring eyes.

The figure raised its head to gaze at me. It wasn't a Gingerbread Girl. It was male, one of the goblins I'd met during my first time in Solitary. I remembered the famished head and raw, scabrous skin. Jesus, I thought, were the horrors starting so soon?

The goblin stood up and approached me. The long, empty sleeves of his nightgown trailed on the floor: it was like watching the ghost of an ape. Then I recognised the gown as the shirt I'd been sewing, which my father had taken away. I didn't like to think how the goblin had obtained that shirt.

The goblin stood in front of me, grinning. His mouth looked black from old blood, and some of his teeth had been pulled, or knocked out. Those that remained were stumps or slivers. 'Pleased to meet you,' he said, holding out a sleeve. His breath was putrid.

'Where's my father?' I demanded.

'Your father?' The goblin looked bewildered, then grinned and pointed to himself. 'He's *here.*'

No. My father had left with Natasha. He'd looked well-groomed and prosperous, and had not resembled in any way the grotesque served up by my imagination who faced me now.

'My father's an architect,' I said. 'He's very famous.'

The creature sighed theatrically. '*I* wanted to be an architect.' Then he sniggered. 'I wanted a daughter like you, as well. You're a nice girl. Not as nice as Natasha, though.'

He laughed, making the cavities in his mouth open again. When the laughter stopped, he wiped away the blood with a shirtsleeve. 'Do you understand or are you stupid?' he asked.

This was a double nightmare. Normality had ended when I started at Aunt Crabtree's – perhaps it had ended earlier. Perhaps it had never been. 'My father,' I repeated stubbornly, 'is an architect.'

'And he's got a lovely girlfriend who doesn't like his

daughter.' The goblin fixed me with his little black eyes. 'Why didn't the daughter run away from school? She's clever enough to get away with it.'

I was ashamed. I'd never thought of running away. The goblin held his face close to mine and the smell of decay in his breath was sickening. 'I'll tell you why she didn't run away,' he said. 'She's in *here*.' With a floppy but violent gesture, he struck his head with both hands. 'With Natasha,' he added, staring at me defiantly.

It was all nonsense. Whatever Natasha's origins, *I* was not the product of some idiot caged in the cellar.

I gestured to the ceiling. 'What about her? Aunt Crabtree?'

He grimaced. 'She did this.' He indicated his bloody mouth, and I felt the point on my arm where Aunt Crabtree had grabbed me. It was reassuringly tender: proof, if I needed it, that I was real.

By now I was hot – so hot that I could hardly bear to talk or think. But I had to talk and think, otherwise the goblin would have taken me over. When he ate my body it had been unpleasant, but at least it had been simple. 'The fire,' I said. 'You didn't do that. I did.'

He nodded. 'That's what I told them, but they don't believe me. They told me that I was seen doing it.'

Speech was taking me further and further into his crazy trap. I felt as if I was looking down into an abyss, and seeing myself at the bottom. I'd had this sensation often at Aunt Crabtree's, and I took it to mean my detachment. The thinking part of me wasn't in the abyss; it was watching. Aunt Crabtree hated my detachment, because it was my protection. I had every chance of surviving this encounter with the goblin, and what would Aunt Crabtree do, what would Natasha do, when I emerged in triumph, uncooked?

I took a short walk around the cellar-oven, testing the walls and the bare pieces of furniture for solidity. The bed was hard and real enough; so was the chair. Both were bolted to the floor, so you didn't damage them, or yourself, in a fit of madness. Best thing to do when the *real* horrors came, was to lie on the floor as still as possible. Sometimes there was a sane and sober part of your mind that could fight the illusion – and while this battle was taking place, stillness and deep breathing were essential.

As I passed the bed, the side of my foot brushed against something small and sharp. I investigated, and found I'd come close to walking on broken glass. One of the Gingerbread Girls had brought it down; concealing it, not very well, under the bed.

I took one of the pieces and tested its edge for sharpness. It was capable of making a clean cut – if I could bring myself to do it. The thought of even slight pain horrified me.

I showed the piece to the goblin. 'I trod on this,' I explained. 'If I hadn't been wearing shoes, I would have cut myself.'

'Yes,' he said.

'So you think I can get hurt?'

'Yes.'

'That means you think I'm real.'

'No.'

No didn't make sense. I could touch myself and I felt solid. If I touched the bruise Aunt Crabtree had given me, I winced. Touching was the only defence I had against his argument. 'You can't say no,' I told him. 'It's not right.'

That was nonsense too. Beyond the Fantasy Door, anything was right.

'You won't feel anything now,' said the goblin. 'Take the glass and try.'

'I can't.'

He grinned, showing his congealing blood. 'It won't hurt.'

'I can't do it.'

'*Try.*'

'No.'

And so we still face each other – daring, sparring. Upstairs, the trained imbeciles couldn't give a damn about who's real and who isn't. Sometimes, in the heat, *I'm* tempted not to care, but I can't let him win. As time passes, he becomes more plausible. Soon, he'll be as convincing as the School for Wayward Girls.

Aunt Crabtree comes down at intervals to bring food and water and to check on the progress of my insanity. Am I cooked yet, like the girls upstairs, or just slightly browned? The goblin thinks she comes to see him. Sometimes, after she's gone, I complain of bruises, and he complains of beatings to his head.

In fact, we're discovering that we have a lot in common.

PEN

G. W. Fraser

The last time I saw Pen was on an evening in May, in the ancient town of Frascati, in the Alban hills above Rome. She walked towards me through the strolling crowds of young men and women. Her red hair fell uncut about her shoulders, in the abandoned style I had once been in love with, and shone, as if she alone had been touched by the sunset.

'Where've all these people come from?' I said, as if it had been just an hour or two since last we'd parted.

'Up from Rome,' she replied, 'to escape the bad air.' Her voice was like mine: calm and matter-of-fact. As if it were a commonplace for us to meet in Renaissance squares, on the worn-down steps of Madonna'd churches, in crowded flower gardens strung with lights, in narrow streets loud with traffic that led away downhill in the evening mist to join the Via Appia on its way into Rome.

She took my arm in the Italian style and we walked without speaking to the nearest café.

'Eight years,' I said, investing those years with so much weight, they dragged my voice down into a feeble whisper. We sat down to take stock, of each other's faces and pavement society. It was like sitting in the catwalk seats at the Milan spring fashions.

'Look at that girl,' said Pen, 'isn't she stunning?'

The last time we'd met, it'd been rainy and grimy. There'd been a busker playing 'Dirty Old Town', while the litter swirled around his feet. There'd been a wide boy selling white handkerchiefs from a cardboard suitcase. We had been fluid creatures then, lacking final shapes; arguing, fighting, hurting, tearing, waiting for our wings to harden in the sun.

Pen, Pen, Pendulum.

I ordered our drinks and Pen gently mocked my business-man's Italian. When she laughed, I was almost glad to see faint lines appear at the corners of her eyes, for otherwise there was no sign on her face of the passage of a time that had hurt me so badly.

'Eight years,' I said again, but it seemed that those years meant nothing to her.

Then, in desperation, I told her my adventures on the Auto-strada. How I got lost on the way to Frascati. How I got lost in the maze of Frascati itself. How, after an hour of fruitless searching, I'd found the only Fiat-sized space in the Lazio region, right outside my hotel front door.

'And then?' she said sweetly.

And then, although in every street, the cars were abandoned like nursery toys, though there were no prohibiting signs or yellow markings that could possibly refer to my modest hire-car, I came out from the hotel to meet her, the only man in Italy who'd got a parking ticket.

'Poor boy,' she laughed, 'you're still the same. Italy will eat you up.'

At nine o'clock, we went to dinner. Pen led me from the busy square to a silent backstreet, to a restaurant where we sat at one end of a long narrow table. Three generations of one Italian family sat at the other end. They approved, with smiles and nods, our selection of Penne alla' Arrabbiata, the fiery Roman delicacy of tomatoes and garlic and peppers, though Pen, in her choice of wine, put on a show of her old defiance. She would not have the local Frascati. She would not have it. She demanded instead a Settesoli white, a Sicilian wine, hinting that the significance of her choice would become perfectly clear, before we arrived at the end of the bottle.

Once, part of the joy of Pen had been watching her get drunk, listening while her talk got brighter and brighter until some outrageous malapropism would signal it was time to take her home. At a party once, in the middle of a general denunciation of organised religion (alias the Baptist Church

of her appalling childhood), she'd begun to talk about the
Opossum Paul on the Road to Damascus.

I wondered: had she been to Damascus? She'd been every-
where else. A postgraduate year in Windsor, Ontario. Then,
for no good reason, nannying to an English family in San
Diego, California. Then a lost year. Then Brussels. Then
Paris. Now, of all things, a technical translator for some
Government Istituto in the science town of Frascati.

Pen and I had never quite lost touch. It would have been
better for me if we had. Her furious letters had come in tor-
rents and trickles. Six pages on the bitter Canadian winter.
An epic tract on the spoiling of children, and on an employer
whom she said was trying to seduce her. Over the years, she
had brutalised her name just as she'd brutalised her hair. Her
signature had shrunk from year to year as she cropped her
hair shorter, in the photographs that sometimes came at birth-
days and at Christmas.

All my love, Penny.

Love, Pen.

Best wishes, P.

Once, part of the joy of Pen had been trying to guess the
way her pendulum would swing. Save the whale or five-inch
high heels? A bluestocking career or the gossip pages? What
would she become?

What had she become?

The first Settesoli was almost finished. The waiter was sent,
under protest, to fetch us another. A pretty little girl of five
or six broke away from the family who were sharing our table
and came to remonstrate with the signorina in her choice of
wine and to gaze up in amazement at the signorina's long red
hair. The little girl, who had ringlets, sat up on Pen's knee
and they chattered away like famous old friends, far too fast
for any man to follow, although after a while it did seem that
they were talking about me.

'You are lucky,' said the little girl. 'You are lucky: he is
handsome.'

Pen laughed and I thought of once-imagined children, little

red-haired scraps, a boy and a girl, sitting like that on their mother's knee, while she told them stories in her scatter-brained way. 'The Little Barmaid' by Hans Christian Andersen. Maybe 'Squirrel Nutkin' by Beatrix Potter.

It was when the waiter brought the wine that Pen came to the point. 'A toast,' she said, slowly raising her glass. 'To all the unworthy people we've ever been in love with,' and my heart, in the warmth of Italy, at once froze over, for fear I was included in her band of outcasts.

I suddenly became angry, in the old, unreasoning way that was part and parcel of loving Pen, but before I could hurt her she said very quietly: 'I never told you I was engaged to be married.'

She might have still been talking in Italian, nineteen to the dozen, for her words seemed to come from another country, one very far away beyond my memories and hopes. The little girl pointed at me from the other end of the scrubbed wooden table.

'Look at the Englishman,' she giggled, 'his mouth wide. open like a fish.'

'Congratulations,' I said, though I could see no sign of a ring.

'Have you ever been to Sicily?' she asked.

'No,' I said.

'It's supposed to be a lovely island. Aldo and I went there in January, to meet his parents. He's from Palermo.'

'Oh,' I said.

I said: 'Is that why you brought me here, Pen?' the old exasperation welling up in me. 'You could just have written.' But Pen had a story to tell. Her head was down. She wasn't listening.

'The airport at Palermo is right on the sea. It's under a mountain. We flew in there late at night. The last flight from Rome. It was raining. It doesn't rain there very often. The road from the airport runs along the coast. We took a taxi and held hands in the back . . .'

I thought: was there any need for her to tell me that?

'The road runs downhill and bends round the cliff and

vanishes in the dark into a narrow tunnel. We were going much too fast. Just as we entered the tunnel, there was an almighty bang from the other end. A lorry had crashed through the central barrier and all the traffic heading into Palermo came piling down the hill and into a heap. Our driver brought the taxi to a halt just in time. But when Aldo and I looked back, all we saw was cars. Spinning as they tried to brake, bouncing from the tunnel walls . . .'

God, I thought, poor Aldo. Poor Pen. I reached across the table to take her hand, to console her, expecting to find her eyes full of tears, but to my amazement, she was smiling.

'They took us to hospital. Bruises and scratches. Aldo met a lady doctor that he'd been at school with, a Palermitano like himself. He got engaged to her instead.'

Pen filled her glass with the last of the Settesoli.

'A toast,' she said, 'to Aldo.'

We walked through the deserted streets for what seemed like hours. The Romans had all gone home to bed. Pen took off her shoes and wanted to walk in a fountain, so I, already an offender under Italian law, had to stand guard nervously till she had stopped splashing. Then, immediately she was dry-shod again, Pen broke a heel of her shoe on a cobblestone, and had to lean on me, the way she used to after student dances, although the stars in the clear hill-top air were like none I'd ever seen in England. Pen told me not to worry about my parking ticket and I said: 'Well, at least you didn't sing.'

In my hotel, we did not need to make love. It was enough for us to lie together again in the same bed, with Pen, the world-traveller, smiling in the semi-darkness the way she'd always used to, whenever she'd exceeded her very small capacity for drink. I went to sleep listing, as I stroked the curve of her small round breast, the things that I thought that we shared and would bind us together. I had passed pride and stubbornness, and was on the way to quick temper, when her breathing and mine merged into one and all the rest was darkness.

In the morning, of course, she was gone when I woke.

*

33

The next time I see Pen, I shall have much to tell her. How Italy, in its inimitable way, ate me up and spat me out.

I had a late flight and a free afternoon. I parked my hire-car near the Colisseum and walked for an hour through the weeds of the Forum. I walked across the city to the Pantheon, the lovely Temple of all the Gods, and found to my disgust it had half-day closing. And when I got back to my car, the back window had been smashed in and my cases ransacked.

Clothes, they didn't appear to want.

Business papers, they maybe couldn't understand.

My passport, ticket and money, I had taken with me.

So, I suppose, it was on a point of principle, that they stole my parking ticket.

The next time I see Pen will be in England at Christmas. I will grant her all the wishes that she made in Frascati, and wrote, no doubt furiously, on the six pages of hotel paper that she left by my bedside. I shall set aside pride, and all the other things that once drove us apart, and forgive her in advance a lifetime's follies, on condition that she forgive me mine, and take her in my arms and welcome her home.

WONDERFUL LAND

Alan Spence

The patterns on the battered desktop made a whole world. Its
varnished surface had been notched and carved by generations of boys, nicked and scraped and inked, initialled as far
back as 1948. But in behind the names, behind the markings,
were the forms, the shapes, that drew me in, the texture and
grain of the wood itself. Here was a flow like tidemarks on
sand, here a swirl like a great eye, here a knot with a ripple
of ellipses round it, like a stone dropped in a pool, like Saturn
with its rings.

Doug nudged me under the desk, brought me back. Where
we were. Last period of the day. Geography. Three o'clock on
a Wednesday afternoon. Grey Glasgow light, out there,
already growing dark.

There was a strange quiet, one or two boys fidgeting, turning round to look in my direction. Old Bryce was staring
straight at me. Waiting.

'Well?'

He must have asked me a direct question. I hadn't even
heard, and now he wanted his answer.

'Could you repeat the question, sir. I didn't quite catch
it.'

'You what?'

'Didn't quite catch the question, sir.'

'Didn't *quite* catch it!' He leaned forward. 'Right. I'll repeat
it very, very slowly. You're listening now? Quite sure?
Right. Tell-me-the-names-of-the-six-rivers-that-flow-into-the-
Humber.'

He might as well have asked me to list the principal exports
of Outer Mongolia, name all the canals on Mars.

No idea.

Doug tried to whisper something to me, his lips tight, a hand over his mouth. It sounded like *Someone*. He changed it to a cough when he thought the teacher had heard him.

'Well?'

'*Someone!*' (Cough)

'Don't know, sir.'

Silence.

'How about *one* of the rivers?'

Doug had given up on me, left me to my fate.

'Does this look at all familiar to you?' said Bryce, indicating a word chalked on the blackboard in square block capitals. The word was SUNWAD.

Sun. Wad. A wad of sun. No sense.

Not a place-name either. Too strange, even for the North of England. Could be East European, Slav. But we hadn't travelled that far. Began with the British Isles and moved round the world in time for the O-Levels in fourth year. Europe, Africa, North and South America. Sunwad. Might have been a moon of Jupiter for all I knew.

Sunwad the Sailor.

The way a word could just look wrong on the page. It had happened the other day with *the*. Turned it this way and that, but the separate letters had come adrift, meant nothing. The same now with this *sunwad*. No meaning. Maybe old Bryce had written it wrong, meant *sunward*.

Sunward the Great Ships. Sunward Ho!

'Well?'

'No, sir.'

'Ever heard of a *mnemonic*?'

Every Good Boy Deserves Favour.

'Yes, sir.'

'Well that's what this is. Something to help you remember. Right?'

'Sir.'

'Write this down. *The six rivers that flow into the Humber are: Swale, Ure, Nidd, Wharfe, Aire, Don.*'

S.U.N.W.A.D.

'Got that? Good. I want you to write it out five hundred

times for tomorrow morning.' He turned his attention to the class. 'Right. Take out your notebooks.'

'Hard cheese,' said Doug, under his breath.

'Thanks for trying to tell me,' I said.

Bryce started drawing a map on the board. 'Copy this.'

Across the back page of my book I pencilled B.A.S.T.A.R.D. And underneath, Baldy Auld Shity Turdy Arsed Rotten Diddy. I showed it to Doug and he grinned.

'A mnemonic!' I said.

'In case we forget!'

I turned to the front of the book, made a start on copying the map.

After school I walked down through town, the shopwindows bright, the streetlights on early, shrill din of starlings above the noise of traffic. I could have taken the subway from Buchanan Street, but I carried on instead to St Enoch. I was taking my time, putting off going home. My father would be working late. He had to take all the overtime he could get. Two nights and a Sunday. The house would be empty and cold.

Our close was at the end of the street. We lived on the top flat, a room and kitchen, three up right. The building still had gas lamps, outside toilets. It had been condemned, would eventually be knocked down, and we would be rehoused in one of the schemes. I turned the key in the door, flicked the light switch in the lobby. But nothing happened. No light. I switched it off then on again, off, on. Still nothing. I thought a fuse must have blown. Then in the light from the stairhead I saw the card on the floor. It was from the Electricity Board. Red lettering. We had disregarded the Reminder and the Final Notice. Now we had been disconnected, cut off.

Through in the kitchen I stumbled around in the darkness, found matches by the cooker, a stub of candle in a drawer. I cleared a space on the table, set the candle down and lit it. The flicker of light brought a kind of warmth. In its soft glow the things on the table stood illuminated like objects in some strange painting. Still life with grubby cups, salt-cellar, milk-bottle, plain loaf, bag of sugar and pile of newspapers. Outside the pool of light, the room faded out to dark in the corners, shadows wavering up the walls.

At least my transistor radio ran on batteries. I switched it on, found Luxembourg, moved the set around till the reception came clear. The Beatles were singing *Money*. The best things in life are free. It held back the bleakness I'd felt closing in. Things could be worse. The cooker was gas. On the mantelpiece was a single shilling for the meter. I could still heat the pie I had bought for my tea. Have it with sixpenceworth of chips. Couple of slices of bread. Wash the lot down with tea.

I checked the coal in the brown paper bag beside the fireplace, a 28lb bag from the corner shop. It was two-thirds full. If I didn't light the fire till after I'd eaten, I should be able to eke out the coal, make it last the night.

I went to the window and leaned over the sink, looked out across the dark back courts. In the tenement opposite, the windows were bright squares, lights burning in other kitchens. I stepped back, saw my own silhouette reflected. I had read somewhere it was bad luck to see your own reflection by candlelight – an omen, like seeing the full moon through glass. I pulled the curtains shut.

I cut across the wasteground to the chip-shop, bought my sixpenceworth, headed back. I held the bag of chips inside my jacket. The heat of it against my stomach was comfort, like a hot-water bottle. My jersey would stink of chip-fat and vinegar but I didn't care. I stopped at the corner shop to buy another candle.

'No something we sell a lot of,' said old Norrie behind the counter.

'Lights have fused,' I said.

'Oh aye.'

'My da's working late. He'll fix it when he gets in.'

'That's terrible that. Boy like you. Supposed to be educated. Canny even fix a fuse.'

I said nothing, managed a stupid embarrassed grin.

'They chips smell good,' he said.

'Aye. I better get up the house before they get cold.'

I turned to go and almost walked into Mary coming in the door. Mary had been in my class at primary school. She was fifteen, the same age as me, but already looked older, had a boyfriend at least eighteen. For years I had sat beside this girl every day. Now being close to her turned me inside out, the half-smile she flashed at me, passing, the scent of her, the way her black hair hung straight and shiny, swung as she turned her head.

'Hiya.'

'Hi.'

Outside I was glad of the cold. It cooled the flush I could feel in my face. In the middle of the wasteground, a group of men had broken up bits of wood to light a fire. They stood huddled round it, waiting for it to catch, passed a bottle from hand to hand. They came from the Wine Alley, the scheme where Mary lived. But the wasteground was their territory, the place they hung about, all hours. There had once been a lemonade factory here. Cantrell and Cochrane. And a row of houses we'd called the Buggy Lawn. All of it had been bull-dozed. High-rise blocks were planned for the site. But for years it had been left like this, a gap, an empty space.

By some kind of sideways connection, I remembered I had a composition to write for English. As if the lines for Bryce weren't enough. The composition was on a poem. Something about windy spaces. And those that toiled in the sweat of their faces.

One of the men was breaking up an orange box for the fire, stamping it with the heel of his boot, then splitting it, ripping the slats apart. He looked across and saw me. He turned and said something to his friend, and they both laughed. The last few yards to my close were suddenly difficult. But concentrating eyes down one foot after the other I made it. Home.

While the pie was heating in the oven I buttered the two slices of bread, put the kettle on for tea. There was interference on Luxembourg – crackling, a high-pitched whine, snatches of a man's voice talking German. So I couldn't hear what music was being played. I cleared a space on the table for my plate, shifted the pile of newspapers. The bottom paper had stuck to something spilled. It tore and left a patch from the back page glued to the red formica. On the torn scrap, two letters from a headline read IF. I tried to scrape it off but it wouldn't come away. I would have to take hot water to it, use a knife. But later. After I'd eaten.

The chips were still just hot enough. I laid a row of them on the first slice of bread, folded it over, bit into it. This was the best thing. The butter melting over the chips, the soft bread, the taste of it all together far back in my throat, on the roof of my mouth. The piecrust was crisp, almost burnt, the way I liked it. The tea was hot, sweet. I swilled it down, poured out more.

The crackling static on the radio suddenly cut. The noises from outer space faded. The German voice shut up. Luxembourg was coming through clear again. Twanging guitars soared over a string section. The Shadows playing *Wonderful Land*. The record was an old one, at least a couple of years.. But I still loved it. I stood up and strutted, did the Shadow-step. Forward, crossover, back, side. I had all the moves down tight, exact, as I played the melody on Hank Marvin's red Stratocaster, bending those notes with the tremolo arm, just the way. I had been a big Shadows fan, knew all their records. I had kept the tunes in my head by putting words to them. *There is a Frightened Ci-ty*. Or *This is a Won-der-ful Land*.

The record stopped. The red guitar vanished. The disc jockey was lost again in a wash of noise, waves of signals drowning him. I was standing in our cold kitchen, in the weird light from a stub of candle guttering on the cluttered table.

Somewhere, at the back of a school jotter, I had Hank Marvin's autograph. Back in summer, the Shadows had been playing at the Odeon. I couldn't afford a ticket, but on my way home from school I'd taken a wander past. Just on the off chance. And there he'd been at the side door, surrounded by people shoving books and scraps of paper at him, to sign.

He looked sharp, in a short leather coat belted at the waist, the collar turned up. Hair slicked back and those Buddy Holly glasses with the thick black frames. I hurried over, rummaging in my haversack, pulling out the jotter. It was all I had, my notebook for Geography. Hank signed his name, wrote *Best Wishes*, inside the back cover, opposite a diagram of the Planetary Wind System.

Bryce had given me a hard time about the autograph. Told me I'd lose marks for defacing the notebook. Asked me who was Honk Mervin anyway. Just showing his ignorance. I didn't care. The autograph was precious.

The only other autograph I had was Jim Baxter's. Slim Jim had signed a photo of himself I'd won in a competition. It had been in the *Evening Citizen*, had really been aimed at adults. I'd only been twelve but I'd entered it anyway, and won. My father had said I was a genius, I took after my mother, God rest her, if only she could see me, she'd be proud, I had brains, I'd get on, get a good education, get out.

The way Slim Jim could stroke the ball with his left foot, flight it accurately over sixty yards, was pure grace, perfection. In the photo he had the ball at his feet, in soft-toed low-cut black adidas boots, the blue Rangers jersey tucked into his shorts at the back but hanging outside at the front. His right arm was stretched out for balance, that left foot poised, drawn back. The picture had been taken in his first game, against Partick Thistle at Ibrox. I had been at the game, in fact I was there in that section of terracing, the blurred background.

The picture was in a frame, still hung on the wall beside the fireplace. I looked across but couldn't see it clearly for the candlelight flickering off the glass.

The competition had been to make up a slogan. Jim Baxter had just joined Rangers from Raith Rovers, but he still had time to serve in the army. Every Saturday they would let him out on leave, to play. The words of the slogan had to begin with the initial letters of SOLDIER. An acrostic. Like Bryce's mnemonic, SUNWAD, to remind me. I had lines to write, and a composition, but later. My slogan had been *Soldier On Leave Devastates In Every Raid*, and I couldn't believe how good it was. But still I'd been amazed at seeing my name in the list of winners. My name in the paper, in print. And a few days later my name again, typed, on the long brown stiff backed envelope that dropped through the door. The postman never brought us anything but bills, no letters, no packages, nothing. So when I heard it hit the floor, I knew it couldn't be anything else. The photo was full colour, glossy, covered with a sheet of tissue paper to keep it good.

I'd taken it to Rangers next home game. I'd waited afterwards, outside the marble entranceway to the stadium. When Jim Baxter had come out I'd pushed my way forward and handed him the photo. And he'd looked at it and smiled, signed his name, with *Best Wishes*. The same as Hank Marvin had written in my notebook. As I'd turned away with the photo, sliding it back in its envelope, a man had grabbed me by the arm.

'I'll buy that off you, son. Give you ten bob.'

He'd held out the ten-shilling note. A fortune.

I'd shaken my head. This was mine, my prize. I had won it. And now it was autographed, it was priceless.

'No.'

'Twelve and a tanner. And that's my last offer.'

He had no idea.

'No.'

The glass on the picture frame was dusty. I lifted it down, breathed on it, gave it a wipe with my sleeve. Where it had hung, a rectangle of wallpaper had been left pale, its colours fresher than the rest.

Down on my knees I raked out the ashes from the grate, shovelled them into the grey metal bucket to be emptied, sometime, in the midden. Then I set the fire. First a few sheets of newspaper, crumpled. Then more sheets rolled up tight, curled and tucked into shapes like doughnuts. Then the layer of coal, shaken out from the bag, spread out carefully, any bigger lumps placed on top. Touch a match to the corners, the edges of the crumpled paper, and watch it catch.

One or two gusts made blowdowns, beat back smoke down the chimney and billowed it into the room. I covered the front of the fire with the blower, a square sheet of soot blacked iron.

Across it I spread another sheet of newspaper, a double page, and the sudden updraught sucked it from my hands as the fire took with a roar. When the sheet of paper started to brown, I peeled it off, folded it small and used it to lift off the blower. The coal had caught and the flames settled back to a steady comforting dance, another source of light as well as warmth.

The knock at the door made me jump.

Nobody ever came to visit. The same way we never had any letters.

The knock was hard, a loud hammering.

My hands were black from the coal, smudged with soot and ash.

It came again. Batter.

I managed to turn the handle with the heels of my hands, so as not to cover it with coal-dust.

There were three men standing there in overcoats and soft hats, like the police.

'Your father in?' said the one nearest the door.

'No. He's working late.'

'Well. We'll have to come in anyway.' He held up a sheet of paper. 'Sheriff's Officers. Your father's facing a warrant sale. For debt. We've got to make a list of all his goods. Put a price on them.'

'What goods?'

'That's what we're here to find out.'

I was aware I was holding my hands up awkwardly in front of me, keeping them away from my jersey.

'Been lighting the fire,' I explained.

'Aye.' Deadpan.

'Well. I suppose you'd better come in.'

'We were planning to.'

Their bulk filled the whole kitchen, made it small. The candle threw their shadows, huge, up the walls and onto the ceiling.

'Light been cut off?'

'Just fused,' I said.

'Oh aye?'

The noise from the radio was suddenly an irritant, a whine.
I switched it off.

'Got that down?' said the man to one of the others who was
scribbling in a notebook.

'The radio? Aye.'

'But the radio's mine,' I said.

'Household goods, son. Got to go down.' He looked about
him. 'Formica-top table. Four matching chairs. Kitchen cabi-
net. Two old armchairs.' He slapped one of them, raised dust.
'Worth damn all.' He pointed to the corner. 'One TV.
Eighteen-inch.'

'That's no ours,' I said. 'It's rented.'

He picked up the candle to look closer. 'One of these coin
in the slot jobs, eh? I couldnae see it right in the dark.' He
held the candle up higher. 'Bed in the recess. We canny touch
that. Or the cooker. That's about it for in here.'

He turned to me again. 'Anything through in the room?'

'Nothing much.'

'We'll take a look.'

He had put the candle back down on the table. I picked it
up and led them through. The draught caught the flame and
it flickered, almost went out. A dribble of melted wax ran
down onto my finger, hot at first but quick to cool and congeal,
form a skin.

Seen in this candlelight, seen by these three men, here,
taking up space, the room was a familiar place made strange.
My bed unmade. Books and papers on the floor. Cold lin-
oleum. A two-bar electric fire, unplugged. A few pictures cut
from magazines tacked up on the wall. Jim Baxter again. The
Beatles. The Shadows. Jane Asher.

'No much right enough,' said the man in charge. 'Side-
board. Chest of drawers. Another manky old armchair. Put
down a tenner for the lot.'

The man with the notebook wrote it all down. The third
man stood looking out the window, across to the wasteground
where that fire was burning, the dark figures gathered round
it.

I took a step to the side so I couldn't see my reflection.

The room was freezing.

'Right,' said the first man. 'That's it. Tell your father he'll be hearing from us.'

I shut the door behind them and stood for a moment listening. They were talking to each other on their way down the stairs, but I couldn't make out any of it.

Through in the kitchen I put the stub of candle back on the table. I peeled the skin of wax from my fingertip. Looking close I could see the wax had taken an impression. My finger had left its print, its unique pattern of loops and whorls. I pressed the wax, rolled it into a tiny ball and flicked it into the fire where it flared with a quick hiss, a spurt of yellow flame.

I raked over the glowing coals, a first layer. I shook on more coal from the bag, rationing it out. My hands were still grubby with dust and ash. I washed them at the sink. The rush of tapwater was icy cold.

I had cleared more space on the table. I had laid out a fresh sheet of newspaper to lean on, so nothing would stick to my papers and books. I had scribbled on the edge of the newspaper with my blue biro, to make sure the ink was flowing. I thought about lighting the new candle. The stub I'd been using had burned low. But I decided to leave it. Might as well use up the last of it.

I would start with the composition. The lines for Bryce were mechanical, dull repetition. I would leave them till later, maybe even do half of them in the morning. The six rivers that flow into the Humber. The composition would take more effort. It would have to be done now. But I couldn't settle to it. I couldn't focus. I sat staring at the candle flame, thinking nothing, mind empty and numb.

Write about the thoughts and feelings evoked by the following.

> This is my country
> The land that begat me
> These windy spaces
> Are surely my own,

ALAN SPENCE

And those that here toil
In the sweat of their faces
Are flesh of my flesh,
And bone of my bone.

No thoughts and no feelings. The only windy spaces I knew
were the gap-sites like the one across the road where the men
from the Wine Alley were standing round their fire. The poem
was about another world.

I picked up my Geography notebook. Inside the back cover
was Hank Marvin's autograph. Best wishes. And on the facing
page, the planetary wind system. The rotation of the earth on
its axis from west to east causes different parts of its surface
to move at different rates. Winds are deflected to the right
in the northern hemisphere and to the left in the southern
hemisphere. Ferrel's Law.

Because we were in the northern temperate zone, the prevailing winds were from the south-west. The windows rattled.
A draught came under the door. The candle flame wavered.
Another gust blew more smoke back down the chimney. The
winds came off the Atlantic. On my map they were blue
arrows, drawn in coloured pencil.

I shut the notebook and pushed it away.

The poem was called '*Scotland*'. I had nothing to say about
it.

I should at least make a start on the five hundred lines, do
something. But I couldn't face it. I was suddenly weary.

The core of the fire now was a good red glow. If I poked it
and stacked coal on top, it would build to a fine blaze in no
time. But it had to last out the night. I shook the bag, picked
out a few more lumps and threw them on. Again I had to
wash my hands at the cold tap. I sat down in the armchair,
held out my hands to warm them. The sheriff's man had said
the chairs were manky, worth nothing. I leaned over and
switched on the radio.

On Luxembourg, Garner Ted Armstrong was preaching
hellfire and damnation, previewing his full-length show on
Sunday. Telling the Plain Truth. He faded out in another

wash of noise, and when it cleared there was music coming through. A couple called Miki and Grif singing *I don't want to go to a party with you. I don't want to go to a dance.* Sweet country harmonies. *I just want to stay here and love you.* I stretched out in the chair. I thought about Mary. I pictured her.

The details were unimportant. What mattered was, somehow, she was here, and that half-smile, and the way her hair, black and shiny, and through to the cold room, the flickering candlelight, the unmade bed, and a sudden draught that blew the candle out and left us in the cold dark, close then touching and clinging together. I lay back in the manky armchair in front of the fire imagining it, working myself up.

I shivered and sat up, not sure where I was. Dark and freezing cold, a hissing noise, a strange acrid smell. My eyes felt gritty. My neck was stiff. Then I remembered. The kitchen. No light. We had been cut off. My father was working late.

The fire was almost out. I must have fallen asleep. The hiss was the radio, the music gone again, lost in space. The last inch of candle must have burned down. I still couldn't place the smell, sharp and burnt and faintly chemical. I stood up and fumbled on the table, I found the other candle, the new one, and lit it. Then I saw the mess, where the smell was coming from. Where the first stub of candle had been. I hadn't thought to rest it on anything. In burning right down it had scorched the table top. It had made a round hole, the formica cracked and buckled round about it, like a volcanic crater.

Krakatoa. East of Java.

'No,' I said, picking off the melted wax. 'Shit. No.'

I had done my best to revive the fire. It flickered away, feebly. The coal in the bag was just about down to the last dross. When my father came home he tried the light switch, not thinking.

'What's happened?' he said. 'No light?'

The way he said it, he knew.

'Been cut off,' I said. 'They left a card.'

He nodded. He rubbed his face. He looked tired.

ALAN SPENCE

'And these men came,' I said. 'Sheriff's Officers. Talked about a warrant sale. Made a list of the furniture. The radio and everything. Said there wasn't much.'

He made a noise in his throat, very quiet, a soft groan, a kind of sigh. He sat down in the other armchair, across from me. We sat there in the unreal light.

'Listen,' I said. 'I'm sorry.'

'What are you sorry about? It's no your fault.'

'No, I don't mean that. It's something else?'

'Eh?'

'I lit this wee bit candle that was in the drawer. I put it on the table so I could see to do my homework. Only I sat here in front of the fire and I must have dozed off.'

He still didn't understand.

'It's burned a hole.'

He stood up and stared at the damage. It was one thing too many.

'It's wasted,' he said. His voice was desolate. 'It's spoiled.'

All of this was years back. My father died long ago. The street we lived in no longer exists.

'What are you thinking?' says my wife.

A few days in London and now we are driving north, back home to Scotland, through the night in this rented car. My wife is driving. My job is to stay awake, make conversation. But it's dark outside and raining hard. The windscreen wipers beat and swish, a steady rhythm. The warmth of the car keeps lulling me.

'You're away in your own head. Haven't said a word for half an hour.'

Half an hour ago I wound down my window to let in a blast of cold air. We happened to be passing a roadside sign that read RIVER SWALE.

'What are you thinking?'

SUNWAD

*

I am back there standing in the room again, in the dark, looking out the window across that wasteground. The place is empty now, deserted. The fire there has been left to burn out. The wind rakes across its ashes, raises a last smouldering glow, a wisp of smoke. The first few drops of rain spatter the window.

The prevailing wind is from the south-west, coming off the Atlantic. Blue arrows on my map of the planetary wind system. Best wishes from Hank Marvin. This is a Won-der-ful Land. These windy spaces are surely my own. I haven't written my essay, or done my five hundred lines. I'll have to take a day off school. Dog it. I'll write a note in my father's handwriting. Please excuse. And oblige. Yours sincerely. His writing is fluid and cursive, copperplate, with here and there a flourish of his own. My father is through in the miserable kitchen, in the candlelight. I imagine him sitting with his head in his hands, wondering how his life could have come to this.

THE SMALLHOLDING
Elizabeth Burns

A woman limps along the marsh road, damp seeping up into her skirt from the wet sedge grass. She clutches a handful of herbs, pulled up by their roots that hang between her fingers like the white tails of mice.

She's tall, nearly six foot perhaps, though the limp makes her lopsided. Her long hair is a tangle of silver, flecked still with its old straw colour, and her eyes, as she glances up from the marsh plants to the sky, are large and pale blue. Bits of damp matted grass, like compost, stick to her coat. They say she sleeps in pigsties sometimes, little grey piglets huddled round her.

She has no home. Her husband died some years ago. His heart gave way, they say. She was thrown out of the smallholding when she let the fields run to mud, and a calf was found starved in the barn. They offered her an old folk's home but she said she'd rather sleep below the clouds. She wouldn't let them truss her up and take her there, so finally they let her be. She shelters in outhouses, begs food from farmers, and is often drunk. She's found an abandoned shed on a bit of dry ground in the middle of a marsh. In winter she has to wade through mud to get to it, but she does it, clinging to sticks while she drags her bad leg though the quag, because inside the rickety shed she keeps her bucketfuls of sloe berries soaking in gin. They say she's an alcoholic. She says it's just to take away the pain. The pain in her foot? they ask. 'The pain in my foot and the pain in my heart,' is what she'll say.

As she came round the bend in the lane, Ginny saw that the light was on. So he was home. She ran the last part, and was breathless as she opened the kitchen door.

Arthur was slumped at the table, head on his arms.

'Where've you been?' His voice was slurred.

'I went out for a walk, it was such a warm night. I forgot the time –'

She looked in the larder.

'There's a bit of bacon here, and I can boil up some potatoes. It won't take a minute.'

She put a pan of water on the stove and began to scrub potatoes. Arthur snored. He'd wake up when the food was ready.

Ginny got the potatoes boiling, and then she remembered the donkey. Arthur was probably too drunk to have seen to it. She went outside, and there was the donkey, still harnessed to its trap, gobbling at the straggly yellow grass in the paddock. Ginny clambered over the fence, bracing herself for the way the donkey would snap at her with its huge dirty teeth as she untied it.

She wanted Arthur to get a motor bike, like some of the other men had these days, or even a van. He said it would cost too much. But there was all this feed for the donkey, and Arthur gave it apples picked from the trees, not just windfalls, and handfuls of carrots that could have been sold at the market. She slapped the donkey's rump, and saw a little cloud of dust fly up.

Before she went back in, Ginny leant against the kitchen wall for a moment – the potatoes wouldn't be done yet – and smelled the blown roses. There were greenfly in the petals, and the bush clambered only halfway up the height of the back door. One day, Ginny thought, rosebuds will trail all over the wall. She smiled, and drew her tongue slowly around her lips. They tasted faintly of perfume. The lipstick. She wiped her mouth quickly, and bit her upper lip. But he would surely never have noticed. She took a last breathful of the flowery air, and went indoors.

Arthur perked up with the smell of frying bacon.

'Good day at the market?' Ginny asked, brightly.

'Not bad.'

'How much did you make?'

He grunted. He didn't like her to know.

'It must have been hot in town,' said Ginny. The fat spattered up into her face. 'It seemed like thunder this afternoon –'

Thunder humming under a tinny blue sky while they had lain on parched ground, miles from anywhere, making wishes, wishes, wishes, her and Tom, this secret man she kept locked up inside her, the two of them making wishes and patterning one another's skin with their lips until they were each as speckled as a thrush's breast with kisses. They lay in the narrow shadow of a poplar tree and heard the whisper of its leaves shaking in the thundery breeze. The insect-clouds above the stagnant ditches stirred. Ginny, so dry and hot, had dipped her finger in the sluggish water: it was warm as a bath, and she'd wished that instead of this she were trailing her hands through cool lake water, lying back in a rowing boat, drifting without oars.

Thinking of how her dress would be crumpling, she rolled onto her side, and felt then the cold metal of the gun against her leg. Tom always had it with him, in case there was anything worth shooting in the marshes, he said. An alibi, Ginny thought. Sometimes the gun frightened her, sometimes on muggy afternoons when the sun thrust down, and she could imagine, peering through the dry bulrushes, the face of Arthur, round and red like the tomatoes he grew against the brick wall of the outhouse. And then, in her imagining, to save her from Arthur's anger, Tom would take the gun and shoot her, and blood would pour from her, spreading a scarlet circle on her dress –

She shifted over into the shadow and closed her eyes. Arthur, in her dream, was running over the marshes calling her name and she rose up like a startled pheasant, her pink dress bright as flapping washing, all the front buttons undone, so that she stood half naked against the skyline, knowing that she should, like an enemy surrounded, hold up a white handkerchief and wave it for surrender under the thundery clouds, but fumbling in her pocket, she could find no handkerchief –

A rook cried out, and she woke suddenly, sat up, and scanned the fens to see if Arthur was in sight.

'Just a dream,' Tom whispered, as she clutched at him, pulling at the skin on his arm with its hairs bleached pale by the sun.

Looking over her shoulder, for Arthur could come from any direction, Ginny saw the shape of a boat against the sky, set high up on the raised canal.

'Will they see us, those people in the boat?' she asked, edgy now, no longer soft and sleepy.

'Too far away,' said Tom, stroking her hot cheeks. 'And no one who'd know us.'

Ginny sank her head back onto his lap.

She remembered then the first time she'd seen a canal like that, the water up above the land, and it had seemed as though the canal could break its banks and spill over and drown her where she stood, down on the level. But Father had taken her hand and they'd climbed up to the edge of the canal and watched as a barge and a boat with brown canvas sails passed by.

Then Father had said they'd need to hurry and get back, because it was getting dark, and before she knew it, Ginny was hoisted up onto his shoulders with her legs dangling down around his neck. It felt as high as a rookery up there, jogging over the bumpy earth, Father's hands gripping her bare legs. She wore white ankle socks and sandals. His hands moved up and down her legs as they walked. Up under her skirt and down to her socks. He said she must be cold. When they reached home and he lifted her down she could still feel the places on her legs where his hands had been. At tea that night he'd called her by her full name. 'Virginia.' Usually he only called her that if he was angry with her, when he got into one of his cold, peculiar moods that Mother said were because of the bits of shrapnel biting into him, and we must make allowances.

But now he was low-voiced and gentle.

'Virginia and I saw a barge, didn't we?' he told Mother, and winked at Ginny.

Afterwards, in bed, Ginny had looked to see if there were any marks, for it felt as if there should be; she still knew where it was he'd rubbed his big hands up and down. She wanted a bath but it wasn't the right day.

Her mother told her that they had named her because of the Virginia creeper on the front of the house they'd lived in when she was born.

'Will you take me there?' Ginny had asked.

So one day they packed a picnic, her and Mother, and rode over on their bikes to see the house. They picked a sunny day, so that the light would be shining on the Virginia creeper, the way Mother remembered it. Bright as redcurrant jam, she said. But when they got there, she said sadly that it had looked better from inside the room, with the way the leaves grew round the window, so that in the morning you'd see them with the light through them while you were lying in bed.

'It was so lovely –'

Then she said, 'Virginia,' very softly and put her hand on Ginny's head and stroked her hair.

'Can we go in?' asked Ginny.

They knocked at the door, but no one came. They stood there looking at the empty house with the bright, fruity leaves climbing all over its walls, and then Mother said briskly, 'Let's eat our picnic now. I know a good place. Your father and I used to go there.'

And they cycled off down a track that led into a wood and sat beside a stream and ate the warm sandwiches and the hard-boiled eggs, grey around the yolks.

When she knew what she'd been named for, Ginny thought of the shapes of the leaves and their ruby colours whenever she had to say or write her full name.

She was big-boned and tall, like her father, who had to stoop so as not to bang his head on the lintels.

Her mother despaired of Ginny.

'When will you ever stop growing?' she'd mutter through a

mouthful of pins as she let down hems. 'You're your father's daughter sure enough.'

A descendant of Vikings, the teacher at school used to call her, making her stand up in class as an example of the Norse race, not Anglo-Saxons like the rest of them. At home she'd be measured against the doorframe, the inches marked in pencil with the date. She'd try and crouch, but Mother always said, 'Stand up straight,' and then sighed as she recorded the measurement.

Sometimes she'd ask wonderingly, 'Wherever did I get such a girl? Why was it you survived and not your brother?' and thump Ginny's glass of milk down in front of her so that it slopped on to the table. 'Not that you should be drinking milk,' she'd add. 'It'll only make you grow more.'

Ginny would pour it down the sink when her mother wasn't looking. Sometimes she'd go down to the river and brew up potions in old tin cans, horrible mixtures with which to poison her parents.

'No looks to speak of,' her mother murmured when Ginny was a teenager, hunched behind a door, listening.

'Her eyes, though,' Father had said, for Ginny's eyes were big and round, the pale blue colour of the sky, a little square of it glimpsed through the barn door during early morning milking.

'Aye, maybe they'll work some magic for her,' her mother said. 'She'll be with us for a while yet, though.'

But then the war came, and Ginny was sent off to be a landgirl at a farm near the sea, where the salty land was clutched back from the waves.

The other girls had photos of soldiers pinned up by their beds, and letters came that they put under their pillows while they slept, and tucked into their underwear while they worked. In the evening they would cluster together under the lamplight, giggling over the creased folds of paper and dreaming of the homes they would set up after the war.

And it came true, for all of them were married, in skimpy

makeshift dresses with one of the other landgirls for a bridesmaid. None of them asked Ginny – they said it wouldn't do
to have a bridesmaid taller than the bride. Ginny went to all
the bright and frugal weddings, and thought that she, so tall
and gawky, would never be married.

So when, at the harvest dance, Arthur Foster offered to
dance with her, she nodded, speechless and pleased. He must
have been ten years older than her – his hair was already grey
round a face red from the sun and the heat of the village hall
– and he was a farmer. After the dance she was breathless and
he brought her a bottle of beer. After the beer, they went
outside and the harvest moon was lying low over the fields,
like a plate dropped out of the sky.

Ginny gasped to see it so big and close. But Arthur only
grunted when she pointed to it, put his arms round her – his
shirtsleeves smelt of sweat – and said, 'Can I kiss you?'

She nodded, because this was what happened under a full
and lovely moon. She was taller than him, and bent her knees
so that her mouth would be in the proper position. It felt
strange to be so close to someone's skin, to see all the little
lines and pockmarks, the places where the sunburn hadn't
reached. His beery breath was warm like a cow's, and his lips
ran with saliva.

That winter she went with Arthur to village dances and
sometimes to the pictures in town if someone could give them
a lift. At Christmas he gave her a pair of stockings. They stood
in lanes on icy nights, and he kissed her and she shivered with
the cold. Back home she would lie in bed and wonder if she
was really in love, like the people in the films.

They were married in the spring and Ginny moved to the
smallholding. The first thing to do was to set about cleaning
up the house. He'd lived no better than the animals, Ginny
found, as she spring-cleaned, brisk and thorough.

'You don't want children, do you?' Arthur had asked her
when the week they'd called their honeymoon was over.

'No,' said Ginny, though she did.

'You'd best sleep in the other room, then,' said Arthur.

Ginny, feeling big and monstrous, used to lie awake on her narrow bed, wondering what was wrong with her. She thought of putting herbs in Arthur's tea, somehow to change him so he would think her beautiful. But it seemed that he wanted a housekeeper, not a wife. Ginny began to dream of a future where Arthur was dead and she was a widow.

Her mother, that summer, wondered what was wrong, but Ginny said everything was fine. Her father, sitting out in the sun with a rug over his knees because the pains were worse, asked her if she was being a good wife to Arthur. Ginny nodded and smiled and did not know what the answer was. Her mother gave her jars of home-made jam that Ginny set in a row on the kitchen windowsill so that they would catch the light.

A sadness grew in her and she did not know how to cure it.

Arthur had lumbered off to bed and Ginny was scraping bacon fat from the plates. When the kitchen was clean, she went upstairs, and sat for a while on the edge of the bed, twisting the rose-pink lipstick up and down in its tube. Her hair and her dress smelt of frying, and her hands were greasy from the dishwater.

It was after midnight when the thunder began, and Ginny lay in bed, counting the seconds before the lightning. Out in the paddock the donkey was braying. Ginny kicked the covers off the bed and pulled the pillow over her head. She began crying silently into the sheets, wriggling her sticky restless body that stretched over the edges of the bed.

She felt too big for the little stuffy room, too big for the flat staring landscape. She wanted to be small and creeping and secret, to live in a place of crannies and rocks and hiding places. Here, nothing was secret: the fields splayed open, acre after acre, and then the salt marshes.

She had a nightmare sometimes where she was fastened to a field, arms and legs spread, pinned like a crucifixion to the bright green grass. Then the field tilted, became vertical, with her body still fixed to it, stuck there for everyone to see.

This was how she felt: so visible, in her strawberry-pink dress against the green, or her sky-blue one in a cornfield. She did not merge in: they could stalk her easily. She would be the one, not Tom, who was found out. She was too big to hide.

The jaggy lightning slanted in through her window, and laid its sizzling eyes on her, Ginny the whore. This was the word that came to her now. She was so scared that they would find out, that Arthur would come running over these tilted fields with a loaded gun –

Oh Tom, what have we done? Was this the reason for the thunder, and the thin white lightning at her bedroom window?

She could work herself into a panic of guilt and sleeplessness like this, twisting these things around. But if she told Tom, all he would say was, 'As long as we're not caught. That's all that matters, Ginny. Keep it a secret, right?' He didn't understand if she told him about dreams and guns and slanted fields with their arms open and all the little hunted creatures, found and shot.

After a while her sobbing stopped. She grew cooler. Her breath came heavily, and she began, slowly, with one finger, to stroke the curve of her breast. She thought about Tom. The thunder moved further away.

She remembered the day he'd come into the kitchen with Arthur. They'd been out shooting rabbits and had a sackful of them.

'Tom's the new man at Windmill Farm,' Arthur had told her.

She had stood with her back to them, sifting tea out of the caddy, and knowing somehow that the man was watching her. She combed her fingers through her hair before she turned back to the table and set down the teapot.

'Catch many?' she asked, looking at the sack.

'A dozen or so,' said Tom.

'Shall I skin one for tonight?' Ginny asked her husband.

'They'll keep,' said Arthur. 'We'll be off to the pub soon.'

After they'd finished their tea, Arthur went off to harness

the donkey. Tom stood at the open back door and said, 'Good-night, Ginny.'

It was nothing, she told herself afterwards, he was just being polite. But none of the men had ever called her by her name or looked at her like that before.

It was a Friday afternoon when he came back. He must have found out that she stayed home on market days. She used to enjoy going into town, and Arthur liked it because she could watch the stall while he went off to drink, and steer the trap on the way home. Ginny would rummage about among the junk, buying little things for the house out of the egg money – an old jug or a sugar bowl, a piece of cloth that would do for curtains. But after a while, she realised that she'd rather stay at home and have a day without Arthur scuffling about in the yard, fussing over the donkey's bran, coming into the kitchen for his silent lunch of cold ham.

Tom had arrived that Friday with a water-fowl for Mr Foster, who'd been more than generous with the rabbits.

'Mr Foster isn't here,' said Ginny. 'He's gone to the market. Aren't you going too?'

Tom shrugged. 'Maybe later,' he said. 'It's my day off. I'm not long out of bed.'

'Thank you for the fowl,' Ginny said, laying the dead bird down on the table. 'It's very kind of you,' she added, as she stood at the sink rinsing the blood from her fingers. She dried them slowly on the rough blue-striped towel that hung on a hook by the sink, and when she stopped, she saw that her hands were shaking. She knew from the way he was watching her why Tom had turned up on market day.

His mouth made her think of raspberries, full and ripe, the way they fell so softly off the bush as you touched them with your fingertip.

It was spring then, when he first started to visit. She remembered how the light had poured through her window, bright as primroses that first afternoon when everything was all yellow flowers and whiteness.

Then summer came, the hot dry summer of dried-up ditches and scant canals, when they lay on the caked mud of river-banks among shrivelled irises with petals turned to paper. Picnics, and her pink lipstick mouth. Once she'd brought a pat of fresh butter for the loaf he'd hack open with his knife, but the butter had melted in her pocket and ran through the paper onto her dress, making a dark stain on the cotton. They'd poured the liquid butter over the bread, and laughed as they ate it. And once Tom had brought bottles of ale – usually they drank from streams, or Ginny would bring some warm milk – and that day Ginny, drunk a little with the ale and the sun and the intoxicating kisses, was able to relax as if no one else in the world existed.

'Gin, though, that's what we should be drinking,' Tom had said. 'That's what your name reminds me of. Did you ever taste it?'

She shook her head.

'I'll make some for you, come the autumn. We'll go and pick sloe berries together –' and he began to tell her of the places where the blackthorn bushes grew.

'Mother's ruin,' Ginny whispered, to the sky, for Tom was not listening.

She had imagined an autumn for them, then – gathering these berries, and others for wine and jam, smelling the blue smoke as the stubble fields burned, finding deserted barns where they could nestle in sweet hay, eating fallen fruit.

Harvest came, and then, in the evenings, the first crisp taste of autumn. There were silky poppies at the edges of the fields, scarlet rosehips on the hedges, reddening apples, clusters of rowan berries. The earth was splattered blood-red, it seemed to Ginny. But not her: she was dry, dry as the juiceless flesh of old chickens. She waited and waited, counting the days on her fingers every morning. No blood, though everything else, it seemed, was turning crimson in a rage of autumn.

*

Ginny knew what she had to do.

She took some cream and butter to a neighbouring farm and swapped it for a flagon of cider. From the gamekeeper, in exchange for some eggs, she got a bit of venison – Arthur's favourite – and made a rich stew. She put on the dress she'd been married in, though it was tight now around the waist. When evening came she turned off the electric light and lit a candle.

'What's all this for?' said Arthur, helping himself to the stew.

'It's the time of year you first courted me,' Ginny reminded him. 'It was just past harvest. I thought we should celebrate.'

'So it was,' said Arthur. 'No need for candles though.'

But he raised his glass of cider, and told her that the food was good.

After they'd eaten, Ginny, her heart thumping, stood behind him, stroking his greasy hair, murmuring to him, so that when it came time, it was easy enough for her to slip into his bed.

'Just this once, Arthur?' she pleaded, and told him it would be safe enough, with the moon shining full through the window. But all the while she was smiling and kissing him – there were bits of meat caught in his teeth – she hated herself, and knew that if she thought of Tom she would weep.

The next Sunday afternoon, while Arthur was snoozing in his armchair, Tom came round for a couple of dozen eggs. Ginny went out to fetch the freshest ones for him, warm and newly laid.

Tom came after her, and stood in the doorway of the hen house, blinking in the dim light. When she'd counted the eggs into the pail, Ginny turned to face him, her hand in her apron pocket twisting her handkerchief.

When she told him, he said nothing, but his lips grew tight with anger. Ginny stepped backwards, further into the darkness with the hens and the straw. The smell in there suddenly seemed unbearable. When she looked up at Tom, she saw he'd taken one of the warm, clean smooth-shelled eggs that she loved to rub against her cheek. He held the egg up for a moment, so that she saw it between his fingers in the light, then smashed it on the ground. Liquid seeped across the trampled earth floor towards Ginny's foot. She stared at it but did not move. Tom let go of the doorjamb and picked up the pail of eggs.

'Friday?' Ginny whispered, urgently.

Tom shook his head.

'You're his now,' he hissed at her. Spittle flew from his mouth. 'You can't have us both.'

Then he turned into the yard and was gone. Ginny stood in the doorway, wanting to cry out, but no sound or movement came. He was halfway across the yard when he suddenly stopped and turned back. Ginny, as though something pushed her from the hen house, ran outside with her arms open to welcome him. But he stopped a few feet in front of her.

'I forgot to pay you,' he said, holding out some money.

Ginny always gave him eggs for nothing; Arthur said the egg money was her business and never checked on it. So now she shook her head, but Tom thrust the coins into her apron pocket, and strode off, swinging the pail. Ginny went back into the hen house and buried her hands under the warm plump body of a mother hen.

The only time she saw him again by himself was when he brought her a bottle of gin wrapped in newspaper.

'Drink it,' was all he said. 'The whole lot.'

After he'd gone, she smelt it and the sweet perfumy scent made her feel sick. She poured it down the drain in the farm-yard and smashed the bottle.

She began going to the market again because she could not bear the long Fridays alone in the house. And there were things to be bought for the child: she found an old cot on one of the stalls, and little coverlets and lacy shawls.

Arthur had been sullen, but less angry than she'd feared,

when she'd told him about the baby. 'Another mouth to feed,' was all he'd said, gloomily. But now, as they meandered home in the donkey cart, he seemed interested in what she'd found that day for the baby. He didn't grudge her the money, either, for that autumn Ginny had made the old apple trees bring in something: she'd picked all the apples instead of letting them tumble as windfalls, and then she'd wrapped each one up in newspaper so that it wouldn't bruise or rot. Now they had sold bagfuls of the crisp red apples at the market, and all the apple money was to be for the baby.

In the winter evenings, as Ginny sat knitting little garments out of white and lemon wool, Arthur talked of how he'd have a son to teach about farming, and how the family name would be not be lost after all. Ginny said nothing.

The child felt like a sack of wheat being trundled about inside her. Her back ached and she slouched around, feeling as enormous and cumbersome as the cow. When it calved that spring, she watched the bloody birth, appalled and fascinated. She felt bloated and ugly, her breasts as heavy as udders, and her stomach too vast for any clothes to fit her except her housecoat, worn without its belt.

The baby, a queer, distorted little thing, died almost as soon as he had been born.

'There's a curse on the boy-children of this family,' her mother told her. 'I hoped it would pass you by, or that you'd have a girl. It never touches the girls.'

Ginny leant over and laid her hand on her mother's. They sat silently for a long while, their hands clasped.

'I thought you'd break the spell, Ginny,' her mother said at last. 'Marrying into another family. We've never had dealings with the Fosters before.'

When she got her strength back after the birth, Ginny began going for walks to tire herself out, so that she could sleep. She walked aimlessly along the lanes, finding hamlets she'd never visited before. She began taking bigger and bigger strides on her long gangly legs, and found she could cover huge distances in an evening. On Sundays she'd easily walk the twenty or so miles to her mother's and back. People stared who saw her striding along the roads, and children whispered behind her back that she was a giantess. Ginny thought she'd train herself to walk to the big towns, the cathedral towns, even the cities . . .

She remembered her old girl's bike. It was far too small for her now, but Mother said, 'Take mine – I never use it any more, I'm too stiff.'

Ginny rode home on the creaky old bike feeling as fast as the wind.

She rode it that winter under leaden-coloured skies that bulged with snow, along lanes where the bare branches of trees crossed above her head like skeleton roofs. She cycled over the marsh roads where the wild geese flew, and on the crusted frosty ground at the edges of fields. Often she was in a daze, pedalling and pedalling to wear herself out. So she didn't notice the ice in the road, skidded, and was tipped into a ditch. The bike lay mangled in the road, and a bone in Ginny's foot was broken. It wouldn't set properly, and refused to heal. The doctor said to give the bike away: she wouldn't be needing it again.

Ginny limped around the yard, spilling milk, tripping over kittens. Everything took longer to do. She skimped on the cleaning of the house – the kitchen floor was covered in muddy footprints and the windows were too grimy to see through – and lost interest in the farm. Uncollected eggs lay cracked in the stinking hen house. Apples rotted in the grass.

The pain shooting through her leg made her snap at Arthur. She no longer glided silently round the house, but banged into things, cursed and shouted. Arthur shouted back. When he came home drunk they used to fight, and he would beat her until her leg gave way and she crumpled to the floor. Often she'd lie there all night, with a blanket dragged over her, and the mangy farm dog nuzzled at her side.

One autumn she collected sloes, hard little berries like beads for a mourning necklace. She burst the skins with needle-pricks, and left the fruit to soak in a jar of gin she'd bought on market day.

She grew to like the strange aromatic taste – she would fling all kinds of herbs into the mixture – for it seemed to blunt the sharpness: of her tongue, of her big, bony body, of the ache in her foot.

When she thought about the past, though, about the man from Windmill Farm, and the baby dead before he'd lived, another kind of ache, sickly and heavy, came over her. But even that could be lifted, she found, as she lay back on bales of hay, slugging the watery liquid from the bottle and letting it blur and soften all the shapes around her, letting it numb the pain in her foot, and the sadness, heavy as slurry, that lay inside her.

THE SEVENTH EGG
Robert Dodds

Magnus held last night's whisky bottle at shoulder height, arm outstretched. Then he released it from his fingers to smash into the others at the bottom of the metal dustbin. The hens reacted as usual, setting up a gust of screeching and flapping in their sordid brutal enclosure. It was half past six. A bitter frosty sun was creeping onto the horizon. Magnus fetched the pail of cabbage leaves, carrot scrapings, crusts of toast and split teabags. Fumbling with icy hands he drew back the bolt of the splintery old gate and stepped into the hen run. The hens crowded around, squawking and jostling and pecking viciously at each other. The mess flew in an arc from the pail and splattered onto the frozen mud and droppings on the ground. The hens rushed at it, claws skidding like ice skates, while Magnus stooped almost double to enter the low hen-house door and collect the eggs. There were seven. Delicately, one at a time, he started to put them into the deep pockets of his baggy tweed jacket. When he got to the last egg, from nowhere the fury welled up inside him like lava rising in a volcano. With all the venom and whiplash that his thin old arm could muster he hurled the seventh egg and then stood in bewilderment while the fury ebbed away as swiftly as it had come. He looked at the yolk dribbling down the henhouse wall. It felt like a small murder.

In the farmhouse Elizabeth lay huddled in the warm protective cocoon of her duvet. She watched the sun's first rays turn the thin bedroom curtain into a screen of light upon which the shadows of the willow tree danced. Her eyes traced imaginary routes along the limbs and arteries of the shadow tree. It had been her dawn game for as long as she could remember –

since she was a little child. Then she heard the baby starting to cry and the milk in her breasts let down in an immediate surge. She threw off the duvet and got her feet half into her slippers. She unlocked the bedroom door and went into the bathroom where they'd put the baby's cot because of the hot water tank. Scooping up the tiny infant she sat down on the linen box and put it to her breast. She whispered to it, confidingly: 'Rosie I'm going to call you. Little darling Rosie.'

Bolting the hen run gate behind him, Magnus turned his steps away from the farmhouse. He picked his way through the rusting carcasses of disused farm machinery that had collected in the derelict stable yard and passed through the gap between the buildings at the corner. The fields lay before him, flat and almost featureless. Fields that Magnus had wrestled with for a lifetime. His eyes narrowed in the bright low sunlight which bounced hard off the frost and dew. His nostrils dilated as he breathed in the cold smell of the earth. Scanning the spiky remnants of hedgerows and the solitary skeletal trees, it seemed to him that there might be an explanation for things out there, if he could only see it.

It was seven o'clock on Magnus' watch when he re-entered the house. Already the suitcases were in the hall. He went into the kitchen. The baby was in its carry-basket by the Aga. He thought it was asleep, but when he leaned over to look in, two eyes flicked open momentarily, disquietingly, before closing again. Tom was curled around the end of the basket. His tail lifted slightly as Magnus rumpled his ears, but he didn't get up. He was old too. Magnus poured his tea from the pot that waited on the Aga and settled into his chair to cradle the warm mug in his numbed fingers. He watched the second hand scurrying around the kitchen clock.

Elizabeth entered the kitchen two minutes later. She paused at the door, taking in the familiar shape of her father's back, the basket with the dog curled around it, the time on the clock. She said nothing, poured her tea, and sat in her own chair at the end of the long table. She hunched her shoulders and tucked her arms into her sides, as if it was necessary to occupy the smallest possible space in the room. She sipped her tea with bird-like dipping motions of her head. She glanced at him, his eyes still fixed on the clock. She waited for some kind of outburst of pleading or fury.

It was a quarter past seven. Magnus got down onto the floor. On his knees. Through the thin lino he felt the uneven old flagstones pressing on his knee-bones. All his joints ached. Tom got up from beside the basket thinking it was a game. Wagging his tail he panted and pushed up against Magnus' chest. Magnus looked at Elizabeth, who stared blankly at him. He felt his tongue lying like a lump of steak in his mouth, immobile. He hung his head. There was no need to speak after all. It was enough to kneel. It was a silent offering of the last shreds of the dignity and bullying pride to which he had clung for too long.

Then Tom nosed into him again, and he lost his balance. He keeled over towards the Aga and put out an arm awkwardly to break his fall. His elbow buckled under him and his head jolted against the baby's basket. He lay on his back on the floor, his head inches from the woven cane of the basket. It rose beside him like a little wall, and on the other side the baby started to cry. Elizabeth towered overhead. For a moment he felt she was going to scoop him up into her arms.

Elizabeth reached over the sprawled figure on the floor and picked up her baby. She would feed it a little more and then change it. By then it would be nearly half past seven. She prayed they would come on time. As she carried the baby upstairs she sang softly to comfort it. The song her own mother used to sing to her: 'It won't be a stylish marriage/ I can't afford a carriage/ But you'll look sweet/ Upon the seat/ Of a bicycle made for two.' The baby's cries turned to gurgling. She bent her head to kiss it, and thought for the hundredth time of how her father must have kissed her thus, on the forehead, as she lay as a tiny baby in his arms.

Tom licked Magnus' face. He pushed the dog gently aside, and looked up from the floor towards the black-painted irregular beams of the kitchen ceiling. His eyes found the nails driven into one of the beams, from which numerous keys dangled on pieces of string, like spiders. There was a key there that he was going to need. Slowly, joints aching, he rolled over onto his stomach and levered himself up with his arms. He felt dizzy at first when he got to his feet, but when the kitchen stopped circling around him he went to the nails and took the key to the gun cupboard. There would be no need for words.

When Elizabeth re-entered the kitchen with the baby it was twenty-five past seven. Her father was back in his chair, his eyes on the clock. Then she saw the twelve-bore propped in the corner by the back door, and the single red cartridge standing like a soldier on the table. She understood the wordless blackmail in an instant. It was how he had dominated her all her life. Until now. Now she was in charge. She felt like screaming at him: 'Do it! Go on – go out into the fields and do it!'

Instead she thrust the baby into his arms and said, 'Here – hold her until I go.' It was done in an instant, without thought. It was the first time she'd let him hold it. Taking the teapot and mugs to the sink she started to run water to wash up. From the window in front of the sink she looked out across the fields. One morning, one long ago morning, her grandfather, Magnus' father, had shot himself out there. It was an empty place – just a corner where three fields met, their sparse straggling hedgerows running together. Once there had been a dark stain there, under a heavy body. A loud report, a flurry of startled rooks, a dark stain. It was before she was born. A part of her childhood mythology. An accident. The gun and the cartridge were there to call up the old story. She looked at the clock. 'Come early! Come early!' she thought. 'Don't ever let me give way to him again!'

Magnus examined the baby. It lay quite still in his arms, eyes wandering unfocussed over his face and on up to the ceiling. It would have a name in due course. Elizabeth and her mother would have it christened, officially or not. It could be a source of hope and joy, like any other child. He was glad Elizabeth had resisted his wishes. And her mother's wishes, once she found out. The image of the seventh egg came unbidden into his mind, dribbling its precious cargo of life onto the henhouse floor. He felt a wave of revulsion, followed instantly by a painful rush of love as he looked from one daughter to the other. His love was forbidden. Destructive. His love brought pain. He looked at the cartridge. Then at the clock.

The clock ticked like a time-bomb. It was twenty-eight minutes past seven. They might come early. Every second that his daughters stayed in the house was like gold dust trickling through his fingers. Why couldn't he hold on to those he loved? One after another they slipped away – his father, his wife, and now his daughter and the new one. He felt panic coming, and thought of the whisky in his room. His arms shook. The baby cried and Elizabeth turned, drying her eyes with the tea towel, and took it back. He put his hands on his knees but they wouldn't be still. They gripped his legs. The knobbly thickened joints of his fingers clung stiffly. His hands were like crabs. They might crawl up, attack. Sweat began to stand on his brow.

Tyres were on the gravel drive. An engine was turned off. Car doors opened and shut. The crabs clung on hard to his legs. His whole body shook. He needed a drink. Now. The doorbell rang.

Elizabeth put the baby into its basket. She looked down at her father in his chair, juddering, shaking, the white knuckles on arthritic hands clamped hard on his legs. She looked at the cartridge, the gun, the threat. She had to decide whether it would all end in whisky, as usual. The doorbell rang again. The door was open, but her mother wouldn't come in. Twenty years ago she'd said she'd never enter the house again.

Elizabeth decided. 'I'll come back, Dad. I'll come and visit you sometimes. I'll bring the baby.' Had he nodded? She wasn't sure. She picked up the carry-basket and went quickly through the hall to the front door.

Magnus stayed where he was, tracing the sound of their movements. Who would have come with his wife – ex-wife? The new man? Not new any more of course. Would he dare? He wanted to run into the hall, fall to his knees again, beg Elizabeth to forgive him, stay with him. But he also needed them all out of the house now, quickly, so he could stumble through the hall to his room. So he could tear open the cupboard door, grasp the neck of the bottle in his teeth and pour and swallow, pour and swallow until fire consumed his tears.

The bags had been carried from the hall. He heard the boot of the car slam shut. The baby crying. The front door shutting, gently, ever so gently. The car tyres on gravel, receding. Gone. Silence. Some rooks.

Later Magnus emerged from the house with the gun under his arm. In his pockets, instead of the eggs, were all the cartridges he could find. The sun was higher now, but his unsteady footsteps still rang out on hard frost as he made his way to the empty place where three fields met.

The deserted farmhouse resonated like a musical instrument to the shots, pair after pair of shots, that Magnus fired up into the empty winter sky.

THE WINNING WAY

Lorn Macintyre

He sprung the catches of the case with his thumbs and unfolded the nightdress, holding it against his shoulders with his dark hands. She noticed how light his nails were.

'Lovely for you,' he said, showing his white teeth.

It had little ribbons hanging from the frilled neck.

'How much is it?'

'Six pounds seventy pence,' he said.

'It's too dear,' she told him.

He looked pained. 'You would pay three times that in a city store.'

She leaned over the table and touched the material. It . seemed to give her a shock.

'All right, I'll take it,' she said, reaching for her purse.

'What's the Gaelic for nightdress?' he asked.

She was so surprised by the question that she had to think.

'*Eideadh-oidhche.*'

She had to repeat it for him.

'*Eja.* It means clothing. And *oychu* is night.'

'*Eideadh-oidhche,*' he repeated solemnly. 'And this?' He took up one of the ribbons.

'*Ribean.* You see what an easy language Gaelic is.'

'Too difficult,' he said, shaking his head as he counted out her change. 'I know one word there's no Gaelic for.'

'What's that?' she asked.

'Me,' he said, touching his chest.

'*You?*'

'Pakistani,' he said.

'Oh but there is.'

He looked confused.

'*Seonaidh am Pacastannaidh;* Johnnie the Pakistani. That's what they call you.'

He showed his white teeth as he smiled.

'You'd better be going,' she said, looking at the clock. Her mother would be coming in soon. 'And don't forget my change.'

He put the coins in a little pile by her hand.

'I wish I could see you in your new *eja* – how did you say it?'

'*Eja-oychu.*'

She held open the door for him.

'*Oidhche mhath.*'

'What does that mean?'

'It means good night. I'll see you in a fortnight,' she said.

'Oh aye, *oychu va,*' he said. He turned at the door, gripping her hand. 'You take care,' he said earnestly.

She stood at the door watching his old van bumping away down the road. He'd been coming to the house for two years, and she bought all her clothes off him because she was sorry for him. But she knew it was more than that as she watched the vehicle disappearing over the rise of the hill. She stood on the step, arms folded, watching the light fade, listening to the hasty pipe of an oyster-catcher at the tide's edge. She was nearly thirty-eight and had worked at the school dinners since she was sixteen. Gaelic hadn't done her any good. She should have gone to the mainland to get qualifications, but her mother was alone.

She was putting the kettle on when she heard the door, but it was too late to take the nightdress through to her bedroom. Her mother was a stout woman with a severe masculine face. Her legs spilled over her shoes, and she had a walking stick which she leaned on as if trying to force it into the ground.

'Is this you buying more trash from the *duine dubh*?' She always referred to him as the 'black man'. She hooked her stick over the edge of the table and held up the nightdress against the glare of the light. 'Damned rubbish. You could spit peas through it. Oh I know where he gets his stuff all right.'

'How do you know?' her daughter asked aggressively as they faced each other over the table. They spoke Gaelic in the house, but most of it seemed to go into quarrels.

'I heard all about him at the Rural. He goes to the Barrows in Glasgow and fills his van up with trash that costs next to nothing, stuff that the big stores put out because there would be an outcry if they sold it. He brings it to this island because he thinks we're all fools. I worked in Glasgow as a girl and I know what good clothes are. Look at this; the label's been cut off it. Bri-nylon,' she said contemptuously. 'You want a good thick cotton to keep you warm in bed.'

'They've nothing better to do at the Rural than gossip,' Cathy said angrily.

'It would do you good to join and learn to make your own clothes instead of wasting your money on buying rubbish from the *duine dubh*. I don't like him, he's got a fly face. I hope you didn't give him tea because you'll have to scald the cup.'

'He hasn't got a disease. He's just the same as you and me.'

But her mother was taking off her coat and hat and sitting by the fire. She hated all foreigners because her husband had been killed on service in Korea, tortured first, she believed.

'I'll take a wee bit crowdie on a scone with my cup,' her mother said.

Cathy was so angry that the scone broke up under the pressure of the knife and she had to throw it in the bin for the hens. She was going to end up looking after an old woman whose weight, moving her from the bed to the pan, would ruin her back. The nearest old folks' home was on the mainland and they made you get on with it at home. There had once been a boy from Barra. He'd come in on a fishing boat. He was fair and quiet, but her mother had deliberately used Gaelic dialect words he didn't know, and he hadn't come back.

She went through to her bedroom and undressed. She put on the new nightdress, standing in front of the mirror, arranging the ribbons at her throat, twirling round like she'd seen the models from Paris doing on the television. It was very pretty, and she felt warm and comforted in bed.

The next night Johnnie was due, her mother was out again at the Rural.

'How did the *eja-oychu* fit?' he asked.

She was very impressed that he'd remembered.

'It's very nice,' she said. But she didn't tell him of the dreams she had when she wore it.

This time he'd brought her a white blouse with a Peter Pan collar, and he held it in front of her, without touching her breasts.

'Beautiful,' he said.

He had such white bits to his eyes, such a ready smile, and she liked his lips.

'Where do you get your stuff?'

He put up his palms, waving them like the member of a chorus line. 'Only the very best,' he said earnestly. 'No rubbish. This blouse would be fifteen pounds in Glasgow. For you, five.' He was folding the sleeves tenderly over the garment.

She paid him.

'Would you like a cup of tea?'

'Now how do you say that in Gaelic?'

She was touched because she knew that he was showing interest in Gaelic for her sake. He held the white scone in his dark hand, biting into the crowdie she'd made herself.

'You'll have to go,' she advised him. 'I have to practise.'

'Practise?'

'For the local Mod.'

'Mod?' he asked.

'It's a kind of Gaelic festival we have every year; I sing at it.'

'Sing for me.'

She was embarrassed, but she stood, her hands clasped, singing the lullaby her mother had used when she was young, a song she'd never heard anyone else singing and which she hoped to win the silver medal with, after all those years of trying.

'You teach me,' he asked, and she went over it with him,

line by line. He stood beside her, singing with her. The inside of his mouth was white and his voice was soft.

'What's love in Gaelic?' he asked when they were having tea.

'It depends what kind of love you mean.'

He put his hand on his heart.

'*Gaol*,' she said.

'*Gul*,' he repeated solemnly. The depth of the word seemed to suit his husky throat. 'And how do you say my love?'

She blushed. 'You're making a fool of me.'

'No, no,' he said, taking her hand.

'*Mo ghaol*.'

'*Mo gul*,' he repeated, looking into her eyes.

This time she put the blouse through in the bedroom before her mother came home from the Rural.

'The walk's getting too much for my legs,' she complained. 'I'll have to give it up.'

'It's good for you, getting out,' her daughter said, alarmed because Johnnie wouldn't call again if she was at home.

'What have you been doing all night?' her mother asked, looking around suspiciously.

But she'd washed and dried the cups.

'I was practising for the Mod.'

'I'll listen to it before I go to bed,' the old woman said.

Cathy stood by the table, linking her fingers and moving her arms, the way her mother had showed her, as if she was singing to a baby.

'Aye, you've fairly come on, you should win it this year,' her mother said. She herself had won the silver medal sixty years before.

The blouse fitted so well over her breasts, and the collar was so neat, the way it lay against her throat, she decided to wear it for the Mod. She was happier at her work, singing as she diced the vegetables for the broth in the school kitchen, stirring the custard with low-fat milk for the children. It was raining the day Johnnie was due.

'I won't go to the Rural tonight,' her mother said. 'The rain's got into my bones.'

Cathy went down the road to the box and phoned the neighbour, asking him to call and offer her mother a lift, though he wasn't to say she'd phoned.

'*Mo ghaol*,' Johnnie called her when he came again.

When she saw what he was lifting out of his case she could feel the heat in her face. His dark fingers were inside the stretched knickers, the way the X-ray had looked when she'd hurt her hand in the school kitchen.

'Lovely on you,' he said.

'Don't be dirty,' she said, though it was making her feel queer.

'What's the Gaelic for knickers?' he asked.

'It's a secret word,' she said.

'Tell me.'

She hesitated. '*Drathars*.'

He repeated it.

'What's love-making?'

He was still holding the stretched knickers.

'*Suirghe*.'

It was a word she hadn't used before, but she knew it.

He repeated it.

'These knickers are specially for you. I only got one pair in Glasgow. They were ten pounds; for you, three.'

She touched them. They had a little red bow on the front. They seemed to give off an electric shock that ran like lightning down through her bones.

'You'd better go,' she said.

'No tea?' he asked mournfully.

'Not tonight. Next time you come I'll have something special.'

'*Mo ghaol*,' he said on the step, kissing her cheek.

She heard his van going away. Then five minutes later it came back. She went to the door, but it was her mother getting helped out of the neighbour's van.

'We passed the *duine dubh* on the road,' she said accusingly. Then she saw the knickers on the table. She snatched them up and tore them apart between her fists, throwing them on the floor.

'The *duine dubh*'s never setting foot in this house again.'

'Then I'll go.'

'You go?' her mother said, rounding on her with her angry precise Gaelic. 'And where would you go? Do you realise what it costs to put a roof over your head, and you earning so little at the school meals? I don't charge you rent; all I ask is a bit of civility and obedience. You know I don't like that black bugger in this house. Giving you these *drathars* shows the dirty trash of a man he is.' The way she pronounced it, she made the word *drathars* sound so ugly.

The night Johnnie was due she made an excuse that she wanted a walk, but she waited at the road end till it got dark.

A fortnight later she took her mother into town so that she could get elastic stockings. She went off by herself. The butcher's shop that had been shut was open again, with a new sign over the door.

SEONAIDH: AODACH
(Johnnie: Clothing)

He was at the counter, talking to a stout woman, and she stepped among the rails of clothes, waiting to speak to him by himself. So this was why he hadn't come to the house the last time: what a lovely surprise, setting up a shop on the island.

His dark hands held the nightdress with the ribbons against the woman.

'*Se stuth anabarrach math a tha an seo. Agus innsidh mi seo dhut, bu toigh leam d'fhaicinn 'se ort, ach dh'fheumainn a dhol a mach air an uinneig nuair a thigeadh do dhuine a stigh.*'

('This is very fine material. I'll tell you this, I wish I could see you in it, but I would have to get out of the window when your husband comes in.')

She couldn't believe her ears. How could he have picked up such fluent Gaelic from his visits to her? Then she understood. He'd been going round the doors of other women, getting Gaelic from them as well. The fly bugger. But she wasn't angry with him; it was because he'd wanted to come and live on the island, to be near her.

Blushing at his Gaelic patter, the stout woman bought the nightdress and went out. Cathy took a deep breath, as she'd done before she'd gone on to the Mod platform to sing the lullaby. She'd worn the Peter Pan blouse he'd brought for her, and as she crooned the song her Gaelic had seemed to come as a new language from deep within her. It had felt as if there was a real baby in her rocking arms.

As she stood among the racks of clothes she arranged the Peter Pan collar to show the silver medal at her throat. She was about to call his name in Gaelic when a woman came out of the back shop. Her head was draped in fine translucent material, and there was a golden pearl at the side of her nose. She was carrying a baby. He bent over and began to sing to it. It was the lullaby her mother had sung to Cathy, and he sang it fluently and with feeling in his soft voice as the dark woman rocked the child in her arms.

Cathy stood among the rails of cheap clothes with the labels cut out. She felt naked. It was worse than being raped. If he'd taken that part of her by force, it couldn't have hurt so much. But he'd taken the Gaelic lullaby, the secret song that contained the only tenderness that her mother had ever shown towards her, and he'd coaxed it out of her for the baby he already had by a woman of his own race. The silver of the medal was cold and heavy on its chain against her throat as she closed the door behind her.

STEPPIN OOT

Janet Paisley

Ah only went oot fur a smoke. Honest tae goad. A smoke. That's aw. Bert's a pal o mine. So ah widnae. It's jist, weel ye kin see in thur windae fae the side o oor hut. An in the daurk, like. Wi thur licht oan. Ah wis jist staunin there, by the side o the hut, huvin a draw it ma fag.

Okay, so ah shoulda moved. Okay. Bit it's bin a while. An they couldnae see me, right? An ye dinnae expect – no wi yer neeburs an them mairrit years mair'n me. No in the kitchen. Wi the licht oan. Christ, ye try no tae think. Bin a long while.

So ah couldnae settle. Couldnae stey there, couldnae go in. Aye right, it hud goat tae me. That square o licht. Burnt in ma heid. That pitchur. Bit ah went fur a walk tae settle masell. It wisnae cauld. The moon wis comin up, big an bonny. Orange. Comin ower the chimney taps. Me in the empty streets, an the moon. S'aw richt.

It bein Thursday, an work the morra, near awbody's in thur beds. Hardly a sowl aff the last bus. Ah'm staunin it the shoap whin it comes up. Mindin ma ain. Listenin tae the quate, cept fur the bus. An Alice Barbour clackin ower the road as it roars awa. She's ower young fur me oneywey. No ma type. Lippy. Hard. A wean jist, bit hard awready. Christ Betty, Betty'd see hur ower the back. She's an airmfu, Betty. Roon in aw the richt places. An wi thick, wavy rid hair that catches the licht aff the fire. Een that open tae ye whin she luks up. Like ye surprised hur. Weel, bin a while, in't it. An efter Bert's? Luk, ah nivir asked fur it. Ah'm staunin there, it the shoap, mindin ma ain. She comes ower.

'Goat a licht?' Cocks hur heid. She's goat blonde hair, cut shoart. Sherp nose. Ah take the matches oot ma poakit.

'Couldnae spare a fag?' She grins, cheeky like.

Ah gie hur wan, an licht it.

'Ye're ower young tae smoke,' ah tell hur.

'Ye think?' She's in nae hurry. She stauns there, blawin smoke oot in a thin grey line. Watchin it.

'Aye,' ah say. 'Stunt yer growth.'

She laughs. A while since ah heard a wummin laugh yon wey.

'Oh, ye think?' she says, shovin hur shouders back, showin me hur chist. Ach, she's young. Bit aw richt.

'Mibbe no,' ah say. Ah'm lukin it hur tits shovin it that thin cloath. Christ, she's gein me trouble, an she kens it. Playin wi me. She steps furrit so's she's pressin oan ma airm. Pits hur mooth up close tae ma ear. Hur braith's warum. Wet.

'Waant a look?' She whispers it. An goes back twa steps intae the close, oot the street licht. Ah go tae.

She's staunin, heid stull cocked tae wan side, swayin hur hips a bit, lukin it me like she's stull sayin it 'Waant tae see?'. Ma fingurs feel thick roon ma fag, hurs playin wi the button oan hur blouse. Unfastenin it. She wets hur boatum lip wi hur tongue, shoves the strap aff hur shouder an pushes hur bra doon. Ah cannae move. Christ, ah cannae move.

She takes a draw it hur fag, then airches hur back furrit so's hur tits luft.

'Ye like lukin, din't ye?' She says. 'Dae ye waant it?' An ah've goat it. Ma airm roon hur, turnin hur heid tae mine, feelin fur hur tongue wi ma ain. An hur tit wi its hard ticht nipple's pressin in ma haun. Christ, bit. Christ! Ah loup awa wi a rid-hoat pain burnin the back o ma wrist, an hur yelpin:

'Whit the fuck ur ye daen? Ye've tore ma claes. Ma brithers'll kill me!'

Ah'm suckin whaur she stubbed hur fag oan me, the bitch. She's puen hur claes oan, puen the teir in hur blouse thegither.

'Ah nivir sayd ye could touch me, ya durty buggar,' she says, an shoves by, heels clatterin oot the close an awa up the road. There's a taste o burnt hair an burnt skin in ma mooth. Tears in ma een. Bloody Barbours. Christ.

Betty's in hur bed whin ah git hame. Ah steer the coal. There's a rid, puckert patch o skin oan ma wrist. Stull nippin.

81

So's ma heid. Made a ful o by a sixteen year auld lassie. Aye, bit ah wantit hur. Stull dae. Christ, whaur am ah comin fae. Ah'm lichtin a fag, tryin no tae think, whin ah hear the gate. Then the thump oan the door.

'Come oot, McDoanald, ur ah'll come in an git ye.'

Ma skin shrinks, crawlin up ma back. It's the Barbours, in't it. Aye, bit ah've loaked the door. An that'll no stoap thum. He thumps again.

'Come oot, ya bastard.' That's Bill. Andra'll be there tae. Christ, yin wid be enough. Ye dinnae mess wi the Barbours. Betty's hauf wey doon the stairs. The weans'll wauken oney meenut.

'Joe,' she says, Quate. 'Whit's happenin?'

Ah think aboot gaun oot the back door. Oot the back an ower the fields. Bit whaur dae ye go, Christ. A place this size. The fist ootside thumps again. Three times.

Betty moves, hur hair's toosled fae the bed an she's drawin hur dressin goon ticht roon hur. Ah huv tae go noo, fur she'll go tae the door. Betty stauns doon fur naebody. Christ, whaur dae ye go. Him ur hur. Ah turn the loak, fling the door wide. Bill Barbour luks up it me, a heid shoarter'n me bit wi the shouders o a bul. Hauns like meat loaf. Andra's leanin oan the gate post. Waitin.

Bill jerks his thumb tae the street. Mannerly. Ye dinnae dae a fella ower oan his ain grund. Yin o the weans girns upstairs.

'Joe?' Betty's askin whit's gaun oan. Christ, there's naewhaur.

'S'awright,' ah tell hur. An ah step oot an shut the door.

ON THE ISLAND
Gillian Nelson

Come with us, they said, do come. It'll be fun. John said, 'It's years since we went away together, Mum.' They combined to press her. Then, suddenly, the subject was dropped. John picked up the newspaper, Annette began to clear the table.

She could see well enough that it was not important to them whether she shared their holiday, or not. If she went, they'd be quite pleased; and if she didn't, they'd have a good time alone.

She had half hoped that John, at least, would say he really wanted her to come. But no.

She did her best to be cheerful, always, but it was hurtful to realise it didn't much matter to her son if she were present or absent. She knew women who complained their families treated them as conveniences – put up with them for baby-minding services, or as knitters. Doris could not say that. Sometimes, perversely, she wished she could, and so have something to feel strongly about. Since Fred died her life was lived in twilight, off thin feelings.

Certainly her daughter-in-law did not need her. Annette was a competent housewife, a good needlewoman, a green-fingered gardener – all this on top of working full-time as a computer analyst. When Doris visited, Annette never found her jobs, or asked favours. If there were children it might be different, but in her heart Doris doubted it. Annette, true to form, would have good babies who slept through the night and would keep them spotless in these peculiar stretchy clothes modern mums went in for.

As John often told her, It's a different world from when you were young, Mum. She didn't need telling. The differences assaulted her in the streets and the shops which were crammed with goods she had no use for and, often, could put no name to. Annette had given her a collapsible basket for shaking lettuce dry. Doris did not find it half as efficient as a clean tea towel. But then you have to dry the towel, said Annette, whereas the basket you can just pop away. She herself had ranks of white cupboards into which she popped everything.

Doris had grown up with rationing and black-out, when thrift was a necessity as well as a virtue. It was neither now, she gathered. Annette called it penny-pinching, with a narrow twist of her lipstick lips. When Doris was a girl you dreamed of looking one day like your mother with a fox fur and high heels. Nowadays, to judge by the shops, grandmas were expected to dress like teenagers. What a turn-round it all was. Yet her world remained like a hidden island in the surging tide of modern life.

Occasionally, when she was out in the town, she would catch the eye of another middle-aged woman as some young thing asked for a commodity unknown twenty years before, (a cream to prevent vaginal dryness, it had been last week, and Doris would have blushed except the girl looked so matter-of-fact), and the older woman would smile at Doris, and she'd smile back and shake her head, feeling a warmth in her breast. Someone of her own kind. She went home and settled by the television happier than usual, until she realised she had not found a friend, only signalled to another soul, adrift on the puzzling tide.

Because she saw so clearly it did not matter to John whether she went with them to Tiree, she decided she would go. The name of the place alone beckoned her. It would be good to leave the city for a week.

On the car journey she sat in the back and slept at first. When she woke they were in the Highlands. Expecting purple hillsides and dramatic crags, she was taken aback by the scenery. The road ran between grey stone walls, too high to see over, or between ranks of close-set pines. It swept through stone villages that crouched under wet hills in the rain, a light, misty, persistent rain. She was careful not to let John see her disappointment. This was not difficult for he and Annette chattered away in front. Once in a while Annette turned in her seat, awkwardly because of the seat-belt, and made a pleasant, informative remark. Usually Doris was miles away and didn't come to in time to hear all her daughter-in-law said, so she smiled and nodded, hoping this was appropriate. Often it was not, and Annette muttered something to John about his mother being past it. Doris heard this perfectly plainly.

The ferry to the island was not large. A lift took four cars at a time down to the hold. In the dining-room they had kippers and oatcakes and strong tea. A voice over the loud-speaker, rolling his Rs just as Doris's elocution teacher had wished her to do years ago, gave out a notice about the four muster points, muster points one, two, three and four. 'Round the rugged rock the ragged rascal ran,' Doris chanted aloud, delighted at the sailor's warm brown voice. Annette looked meaningly at John.

The ship called at other islands before docking at Tiree. They were bare rocky places with wooden piers crusted with limpets. Doris settled her mind to Tiree being another such, as cold, bleak and colourless, and determined not to let John see how let down she felt. She should have gone with her old cousin to Cornwall.

When the ship arrived at Tiree, it was entirely different, really no more than a sandbank. A huge, windswept sandbank thirty miles out in the Atlantic. The waves piled around it. You could look across from the dock and see the far shore and the sea beyond.

They drove to a hotel, a two-storey block beside the sea. John and Annette wanted drinks, more to eat. Doris went to bed.

In the morning the sun shone and the breeze blew the curtains into the room like filling sails. The cleanness of the air she could hardly credit. It was sharp, cool and odourless. It had blown from Newfoundland. She dressed and went out to explore, had to go back for a thicker cardigan, and began again.

The bay curved round in a large easy sweep of sand, and,

backing that, was a wide bank of short grass. Doris found the turf was full of tiny flowering plants. Here and there along the shore, stone houses were dotted haphazardly. They made her think of a child's drawing of a house, with two windows and a door, making a friendly face. The stones at the corners were picked out in white or black paint, the doors were bright colours. A few cottages had wicket fences round them, but most had no boundary mark and stood in the cropped, flowered grass like toys casually placed there, beside diminutive barns and chicken coops. The fowls wandered freely about and so did the sheep and cattle. A dozen or more bullocks were on the beach. They seemed to contemplate the sea's beauty with as much quiet content as Doris.

'You mustn't tire yourself, Mum,' said John when he discovered what she'd been up to, as he called it. 'Yesterday was a long day.'

'You should take more than a cardigan,' said Annette. 'The wind can be treacherous.'

'Isn't the short grass lovely!' said Doris.

'It's called the machair,' they informed her.

'The cottages look like dolls' houses.'

'Crofts. They call them crofts, not cottages.'

That morning they drove round the island. It is not large and the journey did not take long. They saw several more beaches which Doris wanted to explore on foot, but she was imprisoned in the back again.

'Remember your bad hip, Mum. Take it easy. That's what holidays are for.'

No, holidays are for adventures and freedom. After lunch she gave them the slip and walked inland. Here too she saw simple houses, stone-walled fields, and everywhere long views, over gently undulating turf, to the sea. She walked past a small golf course, where only sheep were playing, and came to the western shore. Here was a semicircle of pale sand edged with turquoise water that deepened to blue. There were two long arms of tumbled rocks running into the sea like long jetties.

In the dunes here she met an elderly man carrying fish in a basket.

'Good day,' he said in the clear, lilting voice of the west.

'Did you catch those?'

'Ay, just now.'

His boat lay beached on the shore and his footsteps were cut in the wet sand.

'No one comes here but you,' she said wonderingly.

'Not many,' he agreed.

Doris gazed in delight at the perfection of the beach – the pure sand, the green boat, the rocks, the brilliant water. The man stood with her, silent and relaxed. It was hard to believe she had a house in Anchusa Road, third on the left past the Co-op.

Then the man slightly nodded his head and raised his eyebrows, as if to indicate something. Gingerly she turned. There was a long, low-bodied animal on the dune. It was dark brown, with a whiskered snout, head up, thick tail level.

She breathed a sigh of pleasure.

Then it was off across the dune, down, across the beach, its tiny footprints beside the man's. It plunged into the small waves, showed as a dark skein of shadow for a few moments and was gone.

'Gosh, an otter.'

'Ay. There's quite a few hereabouts.'

At tea in the hotel, Annette was concerned and annoyed that Doris had gone out alone. She said it was thoughtless of her mother-in-law to worry them. They had not been able to settle on the beach and begin the good work of getting a tan. John told his mother about otters, starting with their various types and Latin names, and ending with their sexual habits. If she had let it, this recital might have spoiled the memory of the smooth-coated creature poised on the dune, but she resolutely shut John's voice out.

'She's becoming very obstinate, your Ma,' Annette said to John in their bedroom and he had to agree. 'It doesn't augur well for the future, when we have her to live with us.' This prospect, not as yet revealed to Doris herself, daunted them somewhat but they reflected in silence on the market value of the house in Anchusa Road, which comforted them.

The next morning it was raining but Doris went out all the same in her hooded nylon mac and lace-up shoes. A mist had come in from the sea and every strand of wire, every blade of grass, each leaf was hung with silver droplets. The sea rolled with great care on to the beach as if anxious not to disturb a grain of sand, and the cattle and sheep were motionless, all coated with water, netted by mist. The colours were muted; the crofts had secret faces that morning. The fowls clustered under the fuschia bushes like old women in Fair Isle shawls. It was, to Doris, even more beautiful than the day before. She found a patch of creamy mushrooms with pink gills. She picked one, peeled off the delicate skin and ate it.

Annette was horrified to hear Mum had eaten a wild mushroom, and uncooked too.

'It was one of the nicest things I've ever eaten. It tasted of freedom,' said Doris, unwisely.

'Well, please don't, for our sakes. It would ruin our holiday to have you air-lifted off to hospital with food poisoning.'

The rain eased and the mist dissolved. Another cloudless day came. Annette and John wanted to spend it sunbathing. They insisted Doris came with them. They told her it was foolish all this walking when she usually took the bus everywhere. She'd knock herself up, and then where would they be? Doris began to wonder why they had pressed her to come. It was so obviously a burden to have a wayward elderly mother with them. She supposed they did it to be kind. Then let them finish the job and allow her the freedom she wanted.

'Why does it matter if I walk along the shore out of sight?' She heard her voice becoming pettish and belligerent.

'Oh Mum – because!' replied John impatiently.

Doris remembered how she had spoken to her children when they wanted the impossible, how she too had employed that enigmatic, unanswerable 'because'. Was that how he and Annette saw her now, as a tiresome child with inconvenient questions it bored them to find answers to?

That evening in the bar the young couple made friends with another pair who were keen on sailboarding, in fact could talk of nothing else. Tiree, it seemed, was a great place for their sport. By the end of the evening they had persuaded John and Annette to have a go in the morning. Wetsuits, and boards, all the gear, could be hired.

On the beach there was much laughter, exhortation, shouting, splashy falls, renewed laughter. Doris tried to join in the amusement, but the violent activity made her feel a hundred, and the reverse of jolly, a thorough wet blanket in fact.

She wandered to the end of the beach, round the headland and on. No one called her back. After some time she found she was not enjoying the island views as much as before. She was remembering what John had said about worrying him. She went back.

The two cars that had been parked together by the road end were gone. She could hear nothing but the swishing roar of the waves. A cold wind was suddenly striking her head and shoulders.

The most terrifying ideas came jumping into her mind – John hurt, John in difficulties in the surf, John drifting out to sea and the others rushing off for the coastguard, John *dead*.

Doris began to run along the shore road towards the hotel. It was a couple of miles away, but the nearest place. Her heart pounded on her ribs until the pain of breathing was like knives and her heavy legs would not follow her will. She had to slow, to walk, to walk panting with little spurts of running, and all the time she cried his name in her mind, but wasted no breath on calling aloud.

At the next beach – there they were! Two cars, four people, the boards and sails colourfully scattered about.

'Oh John, John! I was so terribly worried.'

Annette was sharp with her. 'Oh yes, it's all right for you to go off alone, but when *we* do, you work yourself up until you're a candidate for a coronary.'

This time looks were exchanged between four people over Doris's head where she sat slumped, exhausted and faint, on the sand. Annette muttered something quite savage to her husband as she dragged her board back into the waves.

Doris spent the rest of the day sitting in the dunes and 'guarding' their things, like a chastised, painfully good child.

She got no thanks. Absorbed in their new friends and the water sport, John hardly glanced at Doris, and Annette made it her business not to. About six they took the gear back to the hotel and told Doris they'd be back in ten minutes for her.

It was nearly an hour, and growing chilly. Doris kept glancing at her gold watch. It had been her husband's last present. Foolish and untrue to say she always thought of Fred when she looked at the watch, but often the small black face and neat gold numbers did look at her in Fred's way. 'I understand,' it said. 'I like your company. Always did.'

When John eventually came back he explained that he'd had a drink after unloading. 'I knew you'd be content all on your tod here, admiring the sunset.'

'Yes,' she agreed, though she had hardly noticed the sky, being too wrapped up in familiar feelings of loneliness.

After their meal, John settled his mother in the lounge with the television. He said she'd like it better than the bar with them, which was noisy and smoky. She heartily disliked the lounge also. It smelt stale and had a bowl of plastic roses. So she left the television talking to itself and went to her bedroom, where she watched the light fade from the sky over the sea and thought about Fred, and John's childhood; inconclusive, rather useless and painful thoughts.

She expected the last two days of the week to be the same, with her chained to the cars and the sailing gear, but a sea change had come over Annette and John in the night. They seemed to have decided she should be allowed her solitary walking.

'So which direction are you off to today, Mum?' John asked cheerily, and Annette said,

'I think the hotel provides packed lunches, so you could make a real day of it.'

Doris discovered that she resented being told to go out for a walk and leave the grown-ups in peace. This was how Annette made it sound.

'I thought,' said Doris, 'that I'd spend a day on the beach with you. Read my book, write a few cards.'

'There's not the slightest need. You've got your sea legs

now. You must make the most of being here. Back in the city in two days.'

They were off. As she watched their car disappear, the island's charm and colour drained away. Doris stood on the hotel steps, holding her pack of sandwiches, looking at the glinting grey-blue waves. Why had they brought her all this way then? To be kind?

Obediently she set off, walking away from the beaches where they might be sailing. The road led between small fields, the sea visible on both sides over the grass heavy with a night's rain. A ship came into view as if borne on a platform of water, dominating the land as a tower block does a town. When the road ended at the shore, Doris began to plod along the beach. She could not resurrect her joy in the island. She felt herself to be as invisible here now as she often was in the city shops. 'I am wounded,' she said aloud. It did not help to spell it out.

It was a windy day with spells of brilliant sunshine, an acid yellow, which flooded across the water as cloud curtains were blown aside, and then, as suddenly, withdrew. Doris trudged round several bays. In one was the remains of a fire. Painfully she imagined the jolly party that might have gathered there. In another was the bleached keel of a boat, drifted over by sand.

After eating her lunch, she came to the large bay where she had seen the otter, running and swimming, sinuous and dark. If she continued on she would come to the largest sweep of sand where John might be sailing. This she must avoid; had virtually been told to avoid.

Instead, she went out on one of the reefs that extend into the sea like the spokes of a gigantic sunken wheel. It was, perhaps, eight or ten yards wide, partly covered with sand, patches of grass, and trails of dry seaweed. She walked to the far end where the surge of the sea bumped against the rocks and endlessly tossed up small arcs of spray. She looked west over the limitless ocean, not thinking or feeling, just standing and looking.

Out on the reef the wind was chill, so she found a nook of

rocks to sit in and was grateful for the warmth of the sun on her face, neck and hands each time it swooped from behind the clouds. She leant back, her stout legs extended, knees exposed, a woman past her time whom none needed. She was glad to feel hidden in the lap of the sea. A walker on the shore would not be able to pick her out among the rocks.

The water was now grey green, lightly rippled and pocked by the wind, and it heaved with the tide. The currents running through made smooth surface slicks just as the wind will blow paths in a field of hay. She thought of the sea as a water pasture, with wild creatures living in its depths. The old tale that you can sing to seals and bring them out of the sea, came to her mind, and, without self-consciousness or hesitation, Doris began to sing.

She sang in a controlled and confident way. No words, but an Aaah! that dipped, soared, steadied, and soared again.

In less than a minute, a seal's sleek head came up, turned and located her. Then another and another. She sang on, singing like the breeze in trees, or through long, ripe corn.

Soon a dozen dark, smooth heads had risen from the sea, and turned sideways to her. They were the shape of small anvils.

She sang on and on, tirelessly, and saw, as if in a dream or a trance of deep peacefulness, the seals come swimming in towards her. One by one they beached on the damp sand, and remained there at the water's edge, attentive as only wild things can be. A few came up the tiny beach, resting on their flippers.

Doris sang on, her voice as young as a girl's, and as flexible. She sang with a joy she'd forgotten. It was a curiously impersonal joy, as if she were only a mouthpiece for something mysterious even to herself.

The seals were large with solid bodies, gleaming with wet, broad flippers and tails, whiskered snouts. She sensed they were females. Had she stopped singing and contemplated her situation, she might have felt fear, for she was two hundred yards out to sea alone with a crowd of untamed creatures. But thought was suspended in her, as it had been all day since leaving the hotel. She sang on and on, in an unwilled but relentless way, as the tide runs to the land, or clouds are driven over the waves. She sang and the seals listened, motionless.

Perhaps, deep in herself, ideas were forming and being dissolved; but she was unaware of it. When, afterwards, she thought back to this hour, it was to a time of emptiness – herself empty, a vessel through which sound was passing, the sea and the sky empty, the seals reared up in a dark cluster, her singing a communication she was impelled to make but did not understand. Empty, but not lonely. Free, yet part of something indestructible.

She could never say who tired first, herself or the seals. A moment came when she was sitting clasping her bent legs, silent at last, her throat sore, and the seals were slipping down, one after another, into the salty water. The last one became invisible. She remained.

Tired, stiff and bewildered, Doris went slowly back down the reef and across the fields to the hotel, becoming guiltily aware of the time. Fred's watch told her she must hurry, and would not manage a bath before the evening meal.

She prepared a story of sorts for John and Annette, but they asked no more than, 'Had a good day, then, Mum?' before turning back to their sailing talk.

As the tide fills a rock pool, so her emptiness and shock slowly gave way to triumph. She rejoiced in her experience. She felt it had altered her life. If she was a woman who could sing seals out of the sea, well then . . .

Next day they were on the ferry again. The three of them hung over the rail to watch the island disappear, and Doris calmly announced she was going to put 41 Anchusa Road on the market and move to Tiree.

'You'll do no such thing.' Annette was startled into open bad manners.

'Mum, you'd be bored to tears,' said John. 'No shops to wander round everyday. No Mrs Robinson to share knitting patterns with. You'd hate it.'

'What do you know about me, John?'

He stared, not sure whether to laugh at her, or give vent to anger. 'A lot,' he said shortly.

'You don't know the first thing. Mrs Robinson, indeed. Knitting! They are nothing to me, so put that in your pipe and smoke it.' This was an expression of Fred's. The sound of it made her laugh and the laugh became a sobbing snort. She'd be crying if she weren't careful. She swallowed hard. 'Compared to the seals my whole life in the city is nothing.'

'What seals? What are you talking about?'

Annette pulled John aside. 'Look, the poor old thing's overdone. It's all been too much for her. We shouldn't have brought her. It was a nice thought of yours, but really – just look at her.'

Doris was standing at the rail, staring over the sea with a strange expression on her stolid, lined face.

Annette had no need to say what was in her mind, that they were relying on the sale of Anchusa Road, when poor Mum couldn't cope alone, to finance their own move to a much better house in the suburbs. For Doris to buy some godforsaken plot on a lonely island was not part of their plan.

Doris was still at the rail, and seemed to be talking to herself. It made Annette quite uneasy.

When the ferry docked, the car was brought up from the hold. They settled in it and began the journey. Nothing more was said about Doris's crazy plan. Annette and John tried to draw her into their conversation, but she was unresponsive. The road took them back through the grey villages under hills veiled in rain, but all Doris saw, in her mind's eye, was the green-blue of the island.

She felt its tug like the current of the sea, uncaring and implacable.

I EAT MY PEAS WITH HONEY
Georgina McIntosh

Catriona in the next bed kept her eyes shut for the whole of
the first two days. She didn't open them for the psychiatrist,
she didn't open them for her visitors, she didn't open them
for the nurse who came to change the bandage on her arm.
In the middle of the night, when they wheeled her in, she
was crying like a broken heart, clutching that hankie like some
lover back from war. Not that she woke me up or anything
because I'd only been in the place long enough to get the
shroud on, pee in the paper hat and do the quiz. I loved the
quiz.
Had I any:
   false teeth
   hearing aids
   artificial limbs or
   credit cards?
The answers being:
   no
   no
   no and
   ha ha very funny.
Then the biggies. Did I:
   know why I was here?
   have any valuables?
   know what I wanted for lunch?
And in case anybody cares:
   wrapped my brother's car round a tree
   three pound notes, two twenty-pence pieces and an emer-
   ald ring (third finger, left hand, donated by brother before
   I trashed his car)
   steak pie, peas (favourite food of all time) and boiled

potatoes. Yuk to sorbet, yuk to low-fat yoghurt, no to trifle – I'm trying to cut down, thank you.

'Did I pass then?' I asked the nurse. 'Do I get tonight's mystery prize and a chance to go on for the car?'

Ooops. How *not* to make a nurse laugh.

'Are you old enough to drive?' she asked me.

It never fails to amaze me the capacity some people have for crying. Catriona never stopped – even with her eyes shut. Boo hoo hoo. Boo hoo hoo hoo hoo. People who try to top themselves are *so* strange. Like life was so precious that it was worth going to the bother of taking it away.

It wasn't until the third day that she would even speak to anyone.

'Could I have some paper and a pen?' she asked the cleaner.

'I should stick this mop up your tail end, Catriona,' the cleaner said from half under a bed. 'What's a nice girl like you making a mess of herself like that for?'

Well, it was obvious wasn't it: the girl was too poor to afford stationery and, next to shunning the accepted moral and civil codes of society by turning to a life of crime, this was her only way of obtaining Basildon Bond and a first class stamp. I'm in the next bed and I can see all this, right. She gets the paper and stuff, sits about for an hour or so and eventually writes:

1. I have to be assertive enough to ask for more clay.

2. Why is it called a blow job when you're supposed to suck?

I know that. Number 2. I almost said to her too, 'I know that!' but I didn't because I don't suppose I was meant to be reading her 'private thoughts'. But I do. Apparently, if you're *good* at it, you suck really gently until just before he comes and then you blow really lightly on the tip and it stops him. (Of course, it was my brother who told me this so it's him to blame if it's all a heap of crap.) Anyway, it's meant to drive them wild if you do it right. It was driving *me* wild not being able to tell her that I knew it. But that didn't matter for long because she starts crying again – more boo hoo hoo for a bit – then the pen again:

96

ODE TO SAPPHO (DURRELL)
When she was dead, finally
dead
(she hanged herself, you know)
her body left a greater mark   than any man   had made
    on her.

Then she stops, scores it out ('No no save it,' I'm thinking. 'It's genius. It speaks to me.') and then in big enormous writing she scrawls:

DON'T BURY HIM IN THE SAME GRAVE AS ME.

Don't you really hate it when people do that – write *Ode to Somebody-or-other* who you've never ever heard of? And then it bugs you so much that you have to spend four thousand hours trying to find out. As far as I know Sappho was some bint who sat around writing poems while everybody else seemed to be inventing democracy or ouzo or something *useful*. But Sappho *Durrell*? She probably teaches music part-time at the primary school for all I know. That really bugs me that. And what dickhead calls their child after a Greek lesbian? And 'Don't bury him in the same grave as me'? Heavy bevvy.

Then the nurse comes to me for another bucket of the old positively rhesus oh, and I have to shut my eyes because I just can't deal with pain. Especially not mine. Anyway, by the time I can force my eyes open she's got the plot on to the next page:

> My father's the Lord Mayor of London
> He works in the lavvies by night
> He uses his cock to clean toilets
> So Mama gets covered in shite.

Charming. Absolutely *Reader's Digest*. But guess what? I can't stop singing the bloody thing. It's driving me mad. The nurse comes with my dinner and I go:

My father's the Lord Mayor *thank you* of London.

The physiotherapist comes to make an appointment to see me and I tell her:

> He works in the lavvies *I'm not going anywhere, anytime you like* by ni-i-i-ight

Some fart-faced minister goes over to Catriona and says, 'Make like a curtain, Catriona, and pull yourself together,' and I shout over:

> He uses his cock to *Yo! Rev! What would you know about it?* clean toilets la la

And finally two policemen and a doctor tell me I'm alive, brother's dead and the scrap man will give £75 tops for the car and I sing:

> So Mama gets covered in shite.

What is it with hospitals that brings out the singing telegram in everybody? The physiotherapist checks in. She's about two feet tall with a grip like a newborn gorilla and a bedside manner that should have an Equity card. And can she just tell me that I'm going to have to try extra specially hard to move my legs so that eventually I'll be able to get up and away from Suicide's sister in the next bed? No no no. Too much like an ordinary hospital day that one. Death and disability obviously bring out the creative side in everybody else except me.

'You're going to have to help us a bit here, Shelley,' she says, twisting me until I'm sort of back-to-front on myself. 'Right. Let's do it again –

'Legs up! Kick the can
Shelley Scott has got a man
What's his game? What's his name?'
and she points at me:

'He's dead,' I say. 'Better luck next time. Oh look – my legs moved a bit. Are you satisfied? Could you put me back where you found me now?'

I look up and see that Catriona's staring at me. 'Can I have some of that paper?' I ask her.

God knows what I said that for but she gave me some

anyway. She even looked as if she might treat me to a verbal gem from her overflowing wealth of rhyming philosophies but I wasn't for chancing another rendering of Dykey Durrell so I forced myself to ponder the paper with my best 'ah've-a-gotta-paper-an-ah'm-a-goanna-use-it' look on. But paper and me we don't really work that way. Haven't built up much of a foreplay or nothing. I look at it. It looks at me. I sly a look at Catriona. She looks away. Finally I get all giggly on myself and write:

> I eat my peas with honey
> I've done it all my life
> It makes the peas taste funny
> But . . .

. . . then I get bored with it. Anyway, it isn't something profound or anything and somebody else wrote it and bugger-me-softly if I can remember how the stupid thing even ends except that it's something like 'But they stay there on the knife' or another equal banality that rhymes with 'life'. Now, of course, I'm totally pissed-off with being stuck in this bed and everything and I start to stab at the paper with the pen until I get this coolette idea to write:

Get your head out your arse and smell the flowers, babe. And I put the paper on the table in-between us where anybody who happens to look that way can read it if they want to.

Get your head out your arse and smell the flowers. My brother Donald (the dead, deceased, dearly departed one) used to say that all the time.

Get your head out your arse and smell the flowers.

Next thing the shrink's back. But this time Catriona doesn't have time to get her eyes shut because the old sly dog has crept up on us while we're filling in our dietary requirements for tea-time. I'm giving it, 'Gammon steak, (gadzy gadz but anything's got to be better than a plain omelette) peas (favourite food of all time) and greasy-blob chipped potatoes,' before I see that the head-hunter is standing beside my bed and not el loony-tune's. The first thing I think is: This person has a head that looks like a turnip. The second thing I think is, There is a turnip-head speaking to me.

TURNIP-HEAD: Hello, Shelley. Is it OK if we have a little chat?

ME: You've got the wrong bed. I get the singing dwarf for my sorry state. Legs. Down. (I tap my head.) Not up. Down.

TURNIP-HEAD: [to nurse] Can we get her onto a trolley and take her into a side ward?

Well, whaddya know. Two big dudes get the wonders of modern science at their fingertips and the next thing I know *1984* is happening to me.

'This should be happening to you, not me,' I say to Catriona as the waggons roll me west. 'And you can skywrite that in Angel Delight, if you like, *babe!*'

The shrink was this really attractive woman (well, for a turnip-head) with too much blue mascara. I hate women who wear blue mascara. You'd think that someone with that many University qualifications would have the brains to get plain old black like normal people, wouldn't you? So: she's asking me all these loving and caring questions about my parents (who are now both ex-parents due to the female one stabbing the male one to ex-dom just because he beat her around now and again when she spent all his hard-grafted dosh on different coloured shoes and afterwards got her divine come-uppance by breaking her neck when the heel on one of these aforementioned foot fripperies gave way, toppling her down two flights of stairs just before the trial – tragic lot my family, huh?) and all I can think is that she's not the worst-looking turnip-head I've ever seen but that she's wasting a really lovely-looking pair of eyes with this blue shite mascara stuff. God. What a waste of space I can be sometimes. And maybe that's true and maybe that's not but at least I know how to make myself up so that I'll look good in front of other people.

TURNIP-HEAD: You do know that Donald's dead, don't you, Shelley?

ME: It's my legs that hurt not my ears.

TURNIP-HEAD: It's just that you don't seem to be reacting to the news.

ME: [*waving left hand in her face*] Donald gave me this ring.

TURNIP-HEAD: It's beautiful. Do you always wear it on your engagement finger?

I thought this was a strange question for someone who doesn't even know what her own face looks like to be asking.

ME: This is the only finger that it fits. What's up with Catriona?

TURNIP-HEAD: Catriona?

ME: Catriona. You know – the screwball in the next bed. Her old man's been sticking it up her, hasn't he?

She looked genuinely shocked when I said that although, why that should surprise me our dear Lord in heaven only knows. As if she would believe that I could know something that she didn't. As if she would believe me at all. As if shrinks have any clue about anything.

TURNIP-HEAD: I don't think we should talk about Catriona. We're here to talk about you.

ME: I don't need to talk about me. I know about me.

TURNIP-HEAD: But I don't.

ME: Excuse me for being rude (Miss Nedsville stupid-mascara, I'm thinking) but that's because it's none of your business.

TURNIP-HEAD: I'm afraid that it is my 'business' because you were driving the car that your brother was killed in . . . (now she pauses as if she's just realised that she's being overly hard in tone with me. People are so full of crap sometimes, aren't they? Doesn't everyone on the planet just make you want to VOMIT?) . . . and the police can't seem to find any good reason why it crashed into the tree.

ME: The tree threw itself in front of me. It was on a secret kamikaze mission for the Japanese. You not heard there's a Nippon plot to take over the M8 and its subsidiary routes? See. That's you educated types for you. Heads so far up your own arses that you just can't smell the flowers anymore. But: in fact: it is completely true. They really haven't recovered from or, quite frankly, *forgiven* Hiroshima and are, at this very moment, preparing Birnam Wood for a complete takeover of all and every tar-macadamed surface.

We sit and look at each other for a bit. Or, at least, she looks and I frown at the floor and the wall in turn. Then I lie back with my eyes shut and pretend that she's not in the room so that I can feel sorry for myself and cry like an imbecile for what seems like two days or seventeen years or whatever.

I'm burbling a load of crap while I lie there about people who cry on the outside and people who cry on the inside and she says, 'And both feel as if they could freeze the earth over with all that crying – do I know that one!' and I say, 'I'm glad you do because I don't even know why I said it,' and then I start to blubber about that stupid stupid poem-thing, about how it was terrible to make Catriona read it, and she says, 'What poem "thing" is that?' 'I eat my peas with honey,' I say and make it some excuse to cry harder because I can't remember how the knotted thing ends and she says, 'It keeps them on the knife,' and I say, 'Not, "But they stay there on the knife"?' and she says that she doesn't think so and I say, 'It doesn't matter. It's the same difference.' Then I tell her that I hated him because . . . because . . . I forget why because and I ask her if I can take his ring off now and she says, 'Yes,' and I take the ring off and sit up and tell her how stupid I feel and she says, 'It's okay', and holds on to me and I feel like I'm in love with her just because she's holding on to me so gently and then I hate myself because I feel like I'm in love with her. And all her gadzy blue mascara has run all down her face.

Well, a thousand light years later the two big dudes with the wonders of modern science at their fingertips come back to put me back on the trolley that I've just come off.

BIG DUDE 1: That you gettin' evicted already, darlin'?
BIG DUDE 2: She can't have paid her poll tax then, Billy. You been a bad lassie and not paid your poll tax then?

For some reason or other I think this is exceptionally funny and I'm going hee hee hee all the way back to the ward. Then we get there and I find that they've let Catriona out. The biggest fruit-and-nut case this side of madness and they've freed her to make merry with any passing razor that takes her fancy. I just don't understand the thinking of some people, I swear to God. And then I stop thinking about it because what's the point of spoiling my dinner, eh? And then I start to hope that maybe they'll put someone with just a touch of a sense of humour next to me this time. You know, like maybe someone I can relate to a little bit or something.

LAUGHING WOMAN
Frank Shon

During the night he woke up and found her leaning on her elbows in bed next to him, with her face in her hands so that at first he thought she was crying again. But when he leaned over and touched her eyes they were dry. He put one elbow into the pillow and leaned on it, watching her in the glow from the streetlamps outside the window. And for a long time neither of them spoke. Then at last she said, 'It hurts . . .' very quietly and hoarsely, and there was something in this hoarseness that bothered him, something scorched and burnt that outraged him. 'It hurts . . .' Something animal and neutral, so that he almost began to feel guilty again, only stopped himself and felt the outrage grow hot inside him instead. He wished he were alone and that things hadn't got out of hand; he'd hoped it would be cleaner, neater than this. Somehow it had all become entangled, full of chaos, and now the chaos sickened him. He put his arm around her bare shoulders. The quilt had fallen back to her bottom and he could make out the long line that travelled up to her shoulders, down to her elbows, then up again to her hands, which supported her head at the bridge of the nose. He could see her breasts, and the indentation they made in the sheet.

She said, 'You did it; I can see it in here . . .' pressing her temples. 'I know you did.' He sighed heavily, and said,
'No.'
'Yes,' she said. 'You did.'
'Can't you believe me?'
'No,' she said, 'I can't believe you.' And that scorched, burnt neutrality outraged him again. 'I can't believe you any more,' she said, and he wished she were weeping again, because when she was weeping he knew what to say but when

she was empty like this the emptiness was somehow stronger than him, and he could say nothing. He took his arm away from her, just as she said, 'Did she make a lot of noise?' She shifted her weight onto one elbow, and with her free hand reached over and turned his face, which had turned away, back to her. In the half-darkness which she had had time to get used to while he slept, she was looking at him now with a queer smile. 'Did she?' He tried to turn from her again, but she held his chin; and then suddenly he felt the nails begin to tear the skin, it seemed, and roughly, blindly, he knocked her hand away. So that even as he said in a voice that was too loud, too high, 'Cut that out,' he knew that it was already too late to pretend he was merely angry. And in that moment he knew he hated her.

'Did you tell her she had nice breasts, like you always tell me?'

'That's enough,' he said, and she said,

'No, it isn't enough. Did you tell her she had lovely curved hips?'

'I didn't say any of that,' he said.

'Lies. You haven't the guts to tell me. What did you say – that I didn't understand you?'

'Nothing . . .' he said, 'nothing . . .'

'So she never even knew I existed.'

'She knew: I told her.'

'You told her what?'

'That we were all finished with,' he said, and he was pleased because he could feel the impact of the words as surely as a physical blow. She was quiet then, until after a minute she said,

'Well, we're finished now all right; you've killed it, right enough.' She turned away, and put her face in her hands again. 'What a waste it was,' she said, without looking at him. 'All that time . . .' Her voice had lost some of its neutrality, which prompted him to say,

'I'm sorry.'

'Probably you are,' she said, not taking her face out of her hands; 'like one of my children who falls over in the playground and gets his clothes all dirty: sorry because it's all such a mess – not sorry at all really, just put out.'

'If you like.'

'Inconvenienced.'

'Is that what you really think?'

She paused for a moment before saying, 'Yes, that is what I really think. You don't mind lying, but you've no stomach for anything messy, anything with loose ends. I can see you now,' she said, 'scuttling over to her place, looking over your shoulder the way you do, with that nervous little smile of yours.' And she laughed. 'Where did it happen first? Was it her place or did you fuck her here?'

'You shouldn't talk that way,' he said, 'it doesn't suit you.'

'Was it in this bed?'

'I told you before,' he said, very wearily now, 'we didn't.' But she laughed in his face and said,

'Oh, yes, I forgot. That comes later. What does come later, if I'm allowed to ask? Is this the woman to have your babies?' And she snorted.

'I – we don't know yet,' he said.

'No, of course, of course; after all, you don't want to be rushing straight out of one pair of arms into another, do you?'

He felt the hairs on the back of his neck stirring, as if by a cold draught, and he shuddered. 'It isn't like that at all,' he said angrily, reflecting as he said them that he had heard these very words used somewhere before, in a play perhaps or a film, he couldn't remember where . . .

He would have gone on; he would undoubtedly have said all the things he had decided upon and set in crisp but robust sentences when he planned their terminal meeting; all the things he had said aloud to himself as he dressed that afternoon to go out and meet her at their usual spot outside a coffee-shop that had been special to them once. He would have said all of it. But just as he was getting started, something happened that he couldn't have foreseen: she started to laugh. It was muffled at first, like the muffled laughter of a schoolgirl in a church. Her whole body quaked with it, and he could see that she was holding her nose tightly like she always did when she wanted to stop herself laughing at the wrong moment, which was a tendency she had. 'What's the joke?' he asked, but she didn't answer him and even seemed to laugh harder. The hand that wasn't holding her nose was covering her eyes, and she was laughing so hard that he could see this arm shaking and feel it through the mattress.

After a minute he leaned over and switched on the lamp, which stood on a little locker at the side of the bed. It took a few seconds for his eyes to get used to the light, and then he was surprised to find that her face had gone very hot-looking and red; and he asked, leaning very close to her face, 'Are you all right?' But still she never answered him, but only kept on laughing. And the character of the laughter changed, became no longer muffled, because by now she had taken her hand away from her nose so that it was coming out clear and metallic as an alarm. Which was when he started to get scared, and tried to pull her two hands away from where they were stuck now, over her eyes. Only the hands wouldn't come free and he could feel his own face flush as he pulled and tugged at her fingers. She kept on laughing and he kept on struggling, laughing and struggling and laughing and struggling until everything seemed to be accelerating away from them. The picture that hung askew on the opposite wall, the cup with the chipped rim on the little locker by the bed: everything swung away, and he felt nauseous with the violence of it. So that he didn't recognise the voice when he first heard it – did not know it was his own voice saying, 'I'm sorry . . . please . . . I'm so sorry . . .'

THE BEGGARS
Donneil Kennedy

The traffic slows and beggars appear, insinuating themselves amongst the vehicles like searching tendrils.

Beside the car in front there is a leper, an old man in his twenties rotting away slowly and displaying disease as his stock-in-trade. Beyond him an armless veteran leading a blind man, pride and humility in symbiosis. Now, in a flanking movement, scurrying around the wheels, a clan of crab-like creatures, legs wrenched from their sockets in infancy, slaves to an atrophied tradition.

Usually I ignore them. My eyes glaze until the figures are merely shades of horror and soon I see nothing.

This time I am too slow. I have forgotten the children of Niger and a young girl smiles. Copper-coloured confidence tricksters with faces in God's image. They are not an affront to the senses and only my conscience suffers. She smiles again, her face haloed with burnished ringlets.

Once, years ago, I met a young lass of the travelling people on a cool spring morning, south of Lochgilphead. Her feet were bare to the dew, and the air misted round her mouth like a mystical whisper. She had the same fine features, mixing innocence and worldliness.

The tropical sun beats heavily down on the car, and the traffic is at its mid-day worst. Naturally the air-conditioner will overload. Then we will have to switch if off and open the windows. She will reach in and touch me. A little girl stroking the pale skin of my arm with a sense of wonder. No inhibition and no future.

We inch forward and sweat runs down the side of my face. If I had not put Jack's bag in the boot, I would be tempted to change the course of a few lives. He does his deals in cash from a sports bag and he dumped it on me at the building site. It is a cross between a mobile office and a bank, allowing him to do business anywhere. Jack is a chancer. One of the European hustlers this country attracts. Nothing changes, although the colonial version mostly died of fever within three weeks. Nevertheless, he has charm and a good measure of the desperation we all need to come here. I gave him the spare room in my company house and watched in wonder as the trade of a continent switched to my kitchen door.

'Drop off the bag for me,' he says. 'I'm meeting a government secretary and it's a bit naff.' He looks different, face and clothes polished like a crofter on a Sunday.

'No problem,' said I, but I was leave happy – mentally five thousand miles away.

What the hell? Dump it, pick up my case, and off on two months' holiday. The disposal of Jack's bag is a trivial matter.

Just as well it's in the boot. I could get my throat cut just for opening it in public. But Jack doesn't think that way. Once my steward found his famous bag in the shower. Then we spent hours restoring currency with a hair-drier. A minor peril of the cash economy. Money causes worse dangers in 'this Nigeria'.

One day, before the last rains, when the mood of the city was a steam boiler at white heat, I got caught in a riot. It was carefully arranged by the god of chaos, for I was taking the monthly wages to the site at the time. Burning cars, motorcyclists decapitated with iron bars, buildings fired and plundered.

The army had attacked a student demonstration. A girl died. That tragedy was a detonator and the city began to self-destruct.

We sat in the oven-hot car, with a case full of money, waiting, jammed in on all sides. After half an hour the rising tide of noise and smoke told us that there was a new and awesome menace. I looked at my company of three. Myself, John the driver and Ali our old book-keeper.

John reacted first, but quietly. Serious advice that we would be better off on foot and running. Local knowledge is priceless, so we ran. Back the way we came, mingling with frightened crowds, cars abandoned as the panic spread. Like a river of lava the violence caught up and overtook us, but we kept together. At first there was only occasional surprise at a white man with a briefcase, running in the mob. Then the cries intensified and grew together like spreading flames, and we were a rich quarry to be run down and destroyed.

Instinct took us away from the concrete highway, down dried laterite side streets, past tin shacks and crumbling mud buildings, frightened faces, cringing dogs, hysterical chickens. Always unsure if the pounding feet behind were pursuers or pursued. Once I stumbled, almost falling into the open storm drain and the foetid stench mixed with added panic made my stomach heave. It was the reek of my own death, but that thought brought me to my feet again and running hard.

They were fitter than I, the old book-keeper and John, but they did not leave me. We were together in fear. Oddly no one thought to discard the money. That could have saved us, but we were still running down narrow wynds, deeper into the African heart of the town. I remember thinking that terror can be a drug to get high on. Then we turned again, facing a blank wall at the end of the alley. The fear was very real then, intensified, senses heightened so that I could see every molecule in the air, and I could smell it, on myself and my companions.

The morning haze is rising from the city. Dust brought by the harmattan from the Sahara desert a thousand miles away. Cool but menacing. The wind brings meningitis in its clouds and children die. People follow it seeking hope in the coastal deltas and lagoons, migrating like birds to the sea.

The little girl begins to wipe the side window with her ragged sleeve. Her earnest effort makes little difference to the glass but she wants to do something for me. Prove she is worthy of my money. Someone has taught her to do so, on this hard roadside, the only school she knows.

They come from the north of the country and beyond, these light-skinned people. Driven south by the drought that has killed their livestock. They burn scrub and bush for fuel, allowing the endless desert of the Sahel to follow, creeping relentlessly in all directions. Poverty and starvation have brought them to the rain forest, the great city, and the sea. We move again, and the little girl follows. Traders have now gathered like locusts around the crawling vehicles, selling wooden combs, Chinese flashlights, canned sardines.

I wind down the window. Now the outside air feels damp and brings with it the rank sewer smell of the city. It is the stench of poverty.

I can still smell that blind alley where we turned, a place of humble dwellings, its only pretension a television aerial on an iron roof. John, pounding on a door, Ali, facing the crowd. A mob of youths stumbling between the buildings, nervous now they had caught up with us. But the bloodlust was still there. What I saw was the embarrassment of the huntsman before the kill. When the responsibility and dread of being God drives home its own fear and vulnerability.

We faced them, and a stone was thrown. I cursed with such vehemence that some grew afraid, but not enough. Still we faced them. There were more stones, larger now, and a sword was drawn, long evil blade dull red in the afternoon sun. Then knives, for the time of sacrifice was near.

John hammered again and the wood moved. We were through, dragging Ali, and a man screamed at us as he barricaded the portal at our backs.

I knew before we laid his body down that Ali was dead, his skin grey around the bloodied mark on his temple.

We kept vigil behind the barricade until dawn, when the braver taxis began to infiltrate the streets. The man who sheltered us did not want money, but I said my religion required someone to watch over Ali's soul until we could send for his body. Then we stepped out into the growing light and hailed a battered yellow cab.

We sat together in the back, John and I, heading for the city, and the sunrise spread through the windows, warming my arm, scattering orange rays on scenes of devastation. The main thoroughfare looked like part of a city at war and a few bewildered people scraped around the wrecked cars and shattered stores. Some might have been perpetrators rather than victims, but equally confused.

She is still there. Her eyes are just above the level of the sill, one hand feeling the edge of the glass. She looks up and my eyes are drawn deep into my own soul.

We move again. No more than three metres, and she is still with us, hanging on, staring. She must go away. I can stand the smell, and the noise, and the sight of the man-made rotten burrows lining the road, but not this small human being. It is too disturbing to be haunted by the living.

More traders. Tea towels, apples, and – baked beans? The cans are pretty rusty, but they should be fine inside. Hold on! He might just have had some labels printed. Like the Johnny Walker I bought that had sediment in the bottom. I'll bet it was the Yoruba nation who ruined the Phoenicians.

The trader comes closer and I can see that, sure enough, Mr Heinz has changed the spelling of his product. I would be safer buying a Rolex for a fiver. Besides, this time tomorrow baked beans will grow on trees. Jack probably does most of his business in the 'go slow'. Shiploads of steel or containers of dried fish will change hands according to the speed of the traffic.

Looking ahead, past rebuilt Bedford trucks and Lada taxis I can see that something is happening. A checkpoint with soldiers. Searching every vehicle. It's routine. But still I tighten up inside and the sweat chills my temples.

Something is holding my finger. Gently. She is still there.

In the breast pocket of my shirt is a single note. I pull it free and hold it out of the window. Not looking. It is taken from my hand softly – like a caress, and I know that the child has gone, bounding down the line like a young gazelle. There is a sense of loss. Perhaps she was my mascot.

We are ten cars away from the road block. Everyone is showing papers and they have pulled several cars out of the line. I can see by berets and insignia that it is the Brigade of

Guards, an elite corps unused to routine road blocks. One driver is being beaten around the head with a small whip and a Lebanese who looks like his employer is held at gunpoint.

Nobody bothers Jack, damn him, and he goes jogging through bandit country just for devilment. He says the robbers think it's a comedy turn. That is their best quality. Laughter comes more easily than anger.

I can see that John is beginning to sweat now too, and he dries his hands nervously with a yellow duster. He is Ibo, and unlikely to find any friends at an army checkpoint. There is a rumour that he was a senior officer in the Biafran army during the civil war, but he will never talk about those years and the only evidence I have seen are the deep scars on his shoulders, like bullet wounds badly healed. John is a survivor and knows how to keep his mouth shut.

My papers are in order. I'm sure. They must be.

The Lebanese is now being searched bodily, bald head glistening with sweat, large wet patches at his armpit and crotch. His driver lies shaking at the side of the road, clutching his head, tensed against further blows.

I look back now. Partly instinct, seeking escape. I can see that the little girl is trying another car without success. She has no fear, wandering at will, not knowing she has anything to lose.

We are now third in line and I start to look for my papers. My hands are shaking slightly, but we did have a few drinks last night.

So I am not nervous. Not really. If they want to find something wrong then they certainly will, and if I offered money at the wrong time then I would be accused of bribery. You have to pay out large sums to get out of that one. This looks too serious for a money-making enterprise. Everyone is being searched.

There is nothing in the boot but the spare wheel, and . . . Jack's damn bag! Apart from what they'll say about a fortune in currency, I bet he carries other crazy things. Dodgy passports, forged papers, all the chicanery that seems to be his stock-in-trade. What seemed a small favour at noon, could turn out to be ten years in jail.

What would Jack do now? Something bloody clever? He's been locked up more often than he will admit to. I know that. Had to buy his way out heftily a couple of times.

Second in line. A few soldiers are already sizing me up like a chicken they intend to roast. Brass neck and bullshit. There is no alternative.

Most of the beggars have gone now. Drifting down the line away from the soldiers. Only a few children remain, hanging on to good prospects. And there she is. My girl, my mascot. Why? Fast too, she seemed to be fifty metres away less than ten seconds ago.

A corporal drums his fist on the roof. 'Papers!' John hands over a bundle and two black faces peer at me curiously. 'Open!' The fist drums on the boot and I try to look bored as the driver jumps out and scurries to obey. 'Out!' The finger is pointing at me and my time has come. I slide out into the afternoon sun and wait, under gunpoint, as the long blue bag is pulled from the boot. Something touches my hand and I can see the little girl beside me, her hair tingling against the back of my hand.

'What is this?' The corporal is holding the bag aloft. When no one replies his assistant lifts a short, half-metre-long whip and strikes my driver on the face. John stares straight ahead, saying nothing, but the sweat beads heavily on his forehead. An officer is watching silently. He is Hausa. Straight-nosed and arrogant, uniform starched and immaculate.

'It's a bag,' I shout, half laughing, almost hysterical.

'What is in here?' Coloured lights seem to be bursting in my head. 'I don't know. It's not my bag. But go on. Have a look.' My hand is being clutched quite tightly now.

'Is she yours?' The officer speaks, his eyes deep pools, unreadable.

'No.' A soldier makes to strike the child and I push her protectively behind my back.

'These people are thieves.' Contempt, perhaps for both of us.

'Possibly.' I look back at him. Islam allows thieves to have their hands cut off, yet beggars are supported.

'What is in this bag?'

'Help yourself.' I might get away with it. There is a fifty-fifty chance. In fact he hesitates for several seconds. Then he takes the bag from his corporal. Slowly he pulls the zip towards him and I have no tactics left but to stare him in the eye. I can feel John looking at me, sense his horror. John will know he is doomed, for all within range of a crime are guilty.

Carefully then, the officer begins to empty the bag in front of me. Sweatshirt, tracksuit trousers. He pauses, and I can almost see Jack's money reflected in the soldier's eyes as he stares into the bag. Then – socks, underpants, trainers, a towel. All damp and ripe with recent sweat. An odour less repellent than the nearby sewers, perhaps, but pungent enough in its own right. I wait still for the sight of corruption, but the bag seems light and empty.

'You are an athlete?'

'Middle distance.' I lie, but it is a small fiction compared with what I have just lived through.

'Then we will meet.' He smiles faintly, still rummaging in the bag. 'I run for the Nigerian army.' The last object is a stopwatch in a leather case. 'This is valuable,' he says, handing it to me. Does he want it? Is this his price? His face is a challenge and I know he is watching me make up my mind.

'Thank you, Lieutenant.'

'Now you may go.'

'Many thanks.' The object is warm in my hand and I watch him go on to the next vehicle. Beside me the little girl stirs and I see she is looking up at me. 'Here,' I say, handing her the stopwatch with great ceremony. 'Take this. It's a present from Uncle Jack.'

She is grinning through gapped teeth, and I know Jack would forgive me if he could see her face. In a moment she turns, running into the crowd. Then I hear her laughter ring out above the noise of the traffic and it is the true sound of Africa, the joy of life triumphant. It echoes in my head for a long time, and the following silence is mine alone. She has gone forever. Nevertheless I will be looking out for copper-coloured athletes from the edge of the desert in about ten years' time.

As I climb back into the car I notice that the Lieutenant is watching me. He too is Africa, but his cap casts a deep shadow over his features and I will never know what he is thinking.

IN THE GERMAN HOSPITAL
Iain Crichton Smith

Neil was glad that the two of them had managed to get away on holiday, and was not surprised that Angela had left the baby behind with her mother. Angela needed the holiday and so did he. Sometimes – and more especially recently – he had been questioning the very foundations of his marriage. At first he had endured Angela's mysterious illnesses fairly easily, but as time passed and as he himself grew more tired, he had become less patient, less willing to make allowances. Almost certainly she should not have given up her job as a GP – he himself was also a GP – though she would have had to give it up when the baby arrived.

Of course the two of them came from different cultures, he a Scot and she English, he with his perhaps outdated Calvinistic work ethic, and she from a family of brittle brilliance in which, he must face it, there had been a certain instability, as seen for example in her brother Ralph, who had twice tried to commit suicide, even though his results at Cambridge were more than adequate.

He looked out of the window of the plane bound for Jersey. The clouds always reminded him of cotton wool: perhaps because he was a doctor this was not quite a cliché. Angela was asleep and even as he watched her, she trembled. Her pale classic face often looked bloodless, though she didn't have anaemia: he had checked that himself.

'You shouldn't marry her,' his plump commonsensical Scottish mother had told him. 'There's something, well, tense about her.' And during the period of their engagement the two of them had quarrelled bitterly in that normally quiet cottage, vicious quarrels which had shaken the house. Angela would throw things at him, and one night she had a fit. He had thought she was dead, for her breathing seemed to have stopped. She wanted her own way in everything: her will was indomitable, unbreakable. And yet there was nothing physically wrong with her that he could find. Of course she had a lot of time to think now that she had given up her job. The reason she had stopped working was a strange one. 'Why should I cure these people with no future?' she would say. 'I can't stand them.' She had even talked about euthanasia, and old people horrified her. And now she didn't seem to have any maternal feelings for her baby.

I really need the holiday, Neil thought. Recently he hadn't been sleeping very well and found himself getting up in the middle of the night to have a smoke. He hoped there would be good weather in Jersey; he starved for sun. He had been there once as a student and remembered it with affection. Angela had never been there. She stirred again in her sleep. She seemed vulnerable, almost childlike, but there were lines around her eyes. Of course he loved her, even though their turbulent marriage often exhausted him. If only . . . if only she would settle down to the normality that was the fate of most people, except the gifted. She woke, fixing him with a blue eye.

'What are you thinking about?' she said.

She was always demanding this of him: who are you? what are you? as if he was some sort of alien or enigma. She wouldn't leave him alone to his privacy even when he was tired. Who are you? Are you thinking of me?

As students they had been happy; there had been quarrels certainly but these had been dissolved in flowers. It was later that the illnesses, the fits, the restlessness had started. In her there was an extremism, an excess. She simply refused to rest in the common day. She was quite likely to insult his friends with her acid tongue. They didn't like her, and stopped coming. They felt as if they were under examination, and not doing too well. They felt her contempt. She seemed to have the cutting gaze of a surgeon. And then she had given up her job, for the reason she had given him. 'I can't stand these people, they revolt me. There are so many of them . . . they are so . . . less than ordinary.' She grew to hate boils, back-aches, kidney complaints, handicaps of any kind, the smell of age and mortality. The house was kept tidy and clean, almost sterile. She didn't like Neil's comfortable untidiness. She was always jumping up and rearranging the ashtrays, putting the magazines in a neat pile.

She was wide awake now. She suddenly looked at him enchantingly, but slightly mockingly. 'We are almost there, hubby,' she said, glancing at her watch with the black back-ground swept by a green hand, which sparkled on her wrist.

Their evening meal in the boarding house was not appetis-ing. It consisted of naked Jersey tomatoes swimming among pork. The dining-room was also crowded with a number of handicapped people who were on holiday. There was one girl who looked at her watch continually, and proudly announced the time. Angela looked prim and disapproving, but said noth-ing. Neil felt that the holiday hadn't begun well.

In the lounge afterwards he found a newspaper which he looked through in search of entertainment.

'There's a Music Hall show which begins at eight. Would you like that?' he asked Angela.

'Fine,' said Angela distantly. The handicapped group had preceded them to the lounge: one of them had immediately switched on the TV. They were on their best behaviour, polite, neatly dressed. A little man with a cleft palate told Neil it was a fine day.

Angela rose abruptly and went to her room, followed humbly by Neil.

'I suppose I'd better dress up for our outing,' she said ironi-cally, examining her face in the mirror. She had a good face, too, with classic lines and planes. She looked, as always, cool but tense. She put on a green dress which suited her, and by quarter to eight they were seated in the Music Hall with its red stage curtains and ceiling decorated with trumpeting cherubs.

The comedian who began the show wasn't particularly good. He asked the usual questions about where the members of the audience came from: Angela sighed and turned her eyes up in despair. The comedian wore an evening suit which didn't quite fit him, and now and again he would shoot out his cuffs. He told a number of racial jokes, including one about a train driver who had run over a Pakistani on a moor.

'Got him that time,' he said.

Neil didn't like him: neither did Angela. His humour was low, cheap, cut-price, blue, and he wasn't especially funny. He looked as if he had been telling the same jokes for years on poorly-paid circuits. He was followed by a conjuror who produced pigeons, rabbits, spools of toilet paper from a black hat. He did nothing that they hadn't seen better done before.

Then there was a hypnotist billed as the Black Prince, dressed completely in black, looking quite like Jack Palance in *Shane*, Neil thought. He made a fat woman from Yorkshire crawl about the stage looking for an imaginary diamond, her enormous behind like that on a seaside postcard causing howls of laughter from the audience.

'I can't make anyone do what they don't want to do,' he said, as the woman with her huge rump covered in a red dress, stumbled down the steps into the audience again. The hypnotist made a small mild-mannered man attack an actor dressed in Japanese uniform. In the scrimmage his glasses fell off.

Neil was disturbed by the two episodes. It seemed to him dreadful that a man should have such power over others, making for instance a prim woman raise an umbrella in a dry room and stare around her with astonishment when she came out of her sleep. The hypnotist's dangling watch irritated Neil. But he noticed that now and again Angela smiled. She studied the stage eagerly as if trying to work out the hypnotist's secret. She was also smoking rather heavily.

The closing scene brought the comedian back. His jokes were as tasteless as before. A number of scantily dressed girls made suggestive movements behind him, with a mechanical indifference.

When they came out, Neil suggested they go for a drink, as

it was only half past nine. They walked side by side through the balmy evening.

'There was something distasteful about that hypnotist, don't you think?' he said.

Angela didn't answer.

'I mean that sort of power,' he added.

'He was an amateur,' she said contemptuously. 'The whole thing was amateurish. I can't stand that lack of professionalism.'

Stiff and disdainful, she walked beside him.

'The Black Prince,' she laughed contemptuously, 'and all the time he was probably a little man from Wolverhampton.'

And she laughed again. 'Imagine waking up in the morning and finding yourself a fake prince.'

They stopped at a hotel and went in. There was a bored pianist playing some tune that Neil couldn't recall. The room was crowded with holidaymakers. Neil bought drinks for the two of them and they sat at a table at which there was one other (vacant) seat.

After a while the pianist began to play popular tunes and a sing-song developed, with songs like 'Amazing Grace', 'Loch Lomond', 'On Ilkley Moor Baht' At', etc. There was much laughter and clinking of glasses.

A thin middle-aged man in an open-necked shirt asked if he could come and sit at their table, and plonked a pint of beer on it.

'I've got an hour,' he said, 'I start work after that.'

It turned out that he was, of all things, a slaughter house worker, killing pigs for the most part. 'They use guns now,' he said. Neil thought of the pork swimming under the naked skinless tomatoes, and shivered.

Suddenly Angela leaned towards their new talkative companion – who had a French name – and asked him what it had been like during the occupation. Neil looked warningly at her, but her question didn't seem to offend their companion unduly.

'It's a long time ago,' he said, 'I was only a boy. I remember my grandfather had a radio which he hid under a pillow. One day two German soldiers came to the door and said they wanted to search the house. My grandfather wasn't afraid of anyone and asked to see their warrants, and of course they laughed. They found the radio and dragged my grandfather off. He was swearing at them all the time.'

'Is that right?' said Angela, assuming her girlish I-want-to-know-only-you-can-tell-me look.

Their companion gulped down his beer and said, 'There were girls who went out with German soldiers. One man managed to leave the island and join the British Navy before the Germans came. When he came back at the end of the war and found that his wife had been sleeping with a German officer, he cut her ear off. Of course I was only a boy at the time,' he repeated. 'Can I buy you a drink?'

'No, no,' said Neil. 'I'll get you one.' He watched them from the bar as he waited in the good-humoured queue. Angela was listening carefully and now and again nodding her head. She looked relaxed and beautiful and animated, a lovely bird among all the other clacking hens.

Neil gave their companion his pint and sat down again. 'Mind you, we felt we had been abandoned and felt bitter,' said their companion, while a plump woman with a glorious voice sang 'Wooden Heart'.

'My grandfather came back, but he was a broken man. And yet I had seen the day when he had given two German soldiers hell because they killed two of his hens and stuffed them into the boot of their car. Never married myself, I saw too much.' And he stared gloomily into his glass.

'I feel more at ease with pigs, if you'll excuse me, ma'am.' He spoke to Angela all the time and ignored Neil completely.

'But all the same,' said Angela intensely, 'it must have been an interesting experience, the occupation. The complexity of it . . .' Her voice trailed away. However, her philosophising seemed to have bamboozled the pigman, who rose to his feet and said he had to be going.

Angela watched him amusedly as he made his rather unsteady way to the door.

'"My grandfather was a hero,"' she mimicked. '"Told

them off properly." It's all the same. They never know anything or they are all heroes.'

'It must have been difficult for them, all the same,' said Neil.

'Of course,' she said, 'but why can't they tell the truth. Why can't they simply say, "I was a coward, I was petrified." But, no, they stood up against them. The Germans put them in a psychological box and they've been trying to get out of it ever since. Pig killer.'

'You shouldn't have questioned him,' said Neil. 'It's a very sensitive area.'

'Sensitive area, of course it's a sensitive area. That's why I asked. I bet the sensitive area is full of abscesses.'

Her contempt was absolute.

Neil didn't want to argue with her. She seemed to be becoming intense again and he didn't like it. The sing-song continued. The fat women were dancing by themselves in the middle, astonishingly light on their feet. The pianist drank now and again from a pint glass that lay on top of the piano.

'"I told them Nazis good and proper,"' Angela mimicked again, and laughed.

'There were bound to have been heroes too,' Neil protested.

'Heroes, not many, I should think. What I can't stand is the lies.'

The following day they took a bus to the German Hospital. The bus was full of tourists and the driver told them that on the way they would stop for coffee. Neil looked through the green glazed windows at the calm island scenes. There were Jersey cows – rich and sleek – grazing in a field. He saw gardens, some goats, glimpses of the sea. They drove along tree-lined roads. The driver kept up a light-hearted badinage with the passengers.

On the seat behind Angela and Neil an old woman kept asking querulously, 'When are we going to stop for our coffee?' She had a high quavering voice. However, when they arrived at the restaurant, it wasn't open.

'Sorry about that,' said the driver, 'we'll stop on our way back.'

'Oo, hasn't he a nice body,' said a large woman who sat beside a small grey-haired man.

The bus wound its way along quiet roads and the leaves rustled against the roof.

They eventually stopped at the hospital and queued for tickets.

Neil felt a chill run through his body as they entered. There was a pile of stones – for the hospital hadn't been finished – with names carved on them.

'It was built by Russian slave labour,' he told Angela, glancing at the brochure he had bought. The names on the stones filled him with horror. He saw the prisoners carving them as a last memorial to their lives.

They walked along corridors, suddenly stunned at a corner by what seemed to be a German soldier who stood there with a rifle in his hand, impassive, commanding. It was of course a dummy in green uniform who still, however, looked imperious and frightening.

They came to a room in which there were a large number of documents, photographs, and even letters from the time of the occupation. One of the letters was anonymous and told the commandant of a woman who kept a radio and listened to British broadcasts.

'They obviously paid off old scores,' said Neil. The island had probably seethed with rancour, betrayal and evil. Commandos too were betrayed. A huge red flag had to be laid down to be seen from the air and show that the island had surrendered. But there must have been heroes, he thought, there must have been. There always are.

They looked in at a room in which the Germans had sat and relaxed. There were some books, a scattering of old German magazines on the table, and German music playing from an old-fashioned wireless. Neil could imagine them stretching their legs out and leafing over the pages of a magazine. The room was not well lit and the dummies looked real people. It had a curious musty eeriness about it.

Another room was obviously an operating room. The instruments looked old and almost primitive. There were dummy surgeons here and dummy nurses.

Neil happened at that moment to turn and look at Angela: she was staring into the room with a kind of ecstasy. Her mouth was open and she was breathing quickly. Oh, my God, he thought, this is the face of a German woman doctor, one of the ones he had seen either here or in a photograph. And in a blinding moment he saw it; this is what she had been starving for, this extremism. He stared at the operating table, the dusty instruments, and he could see the operation being performed by a man dressed in a green apron and wearing gloves: operations on those who had to be corrected of handicap, the sick, the unfit, the ones who were less than competent.

A terrifying lock in the cell door clicked into place. The hypnotist they had seen the previous night became Hitler himself, moustached, shabby, the Black Prince, the evil one. The cold chilled his bones.

The Germans had been preparing to build a gas chamber, according to the brochure: the pipes were there but were not joined properly. It was only the Allied victory that had prevented them.

Angela stood almost as if in a trance staring into the cell. Poor, poor Angela, he thought. Born in the wrong place at the wrong time. Looking for extremism, for the cleanliness of the absolute, sick for a world she didn't know, hating the pathetic ones with their diseases and their handicaps. Those without aim, without future, without significant history. At the end of the corridor he saw another helmeted German soldier caught eternally in the half darkness, an abhorrent green monster. Neil felt as if he was in prison, as if he was being throttled. He had a sudden longing for daylight, for ordinariness.

'Come on,' he said, 'we're late,' pushing Angela ahead of him. They made their way to the exit. The other passengers were already in the bus looking disapproving.

They climbed the steps and took their seats guiltily, and the bus set off through the blazing light and heat. Angela was looking through the window dazedly. My love, my love, thought Neil, so this was your sickness, this longing for the excessive, the unlawful, the absolute correction: this yearning for the successful and the handsome that exists only in a diseased imagination. Horror, horror, such horror.

Out of his dreams of contempt and terror he heard the ancient woman mumble, 'When do we get our coffee?'

The driver said we would stop for a coffee; her suffering daughter said, as if she was speaking to a child, 'It won't be long now, it won't be long.'

THE BUTTERFLY

Willie Orr

She did not cry. She fed the stirks, let the cows out to the hill and returned to the house to clear out his room, stripping the bed to the horsehair mattress and bundling his belongings into a sack. She never went to prayer meetings again nor into the village. She sold the beasts and gradually ragwort and thistles took over the rigs.

Donald Alec finished the tile drains in the laird's meadow. With his legs astride the deep slit in the soil, he cleared the last few inches at the bottom, pushing the long-handled shovel ahead of him through the earth. Its narrow blade slid sensuously into the clay, leaving a rounded channel in which the drain tiles would fit neatly. He worked mechanically, not thinking about the drains but planning his evening. Every Wednesday his mother left the house to attend the prayer meeting and he was left alone. Wednesday, therefore, was precious.

He reached the end of the drain and stood for a moment, gazing over the stone dyke at the hard slate sea and basalt sky. With his boots planted in the loose earth and his small, round, wrinkled face as still as the rocks in the head-rig, he seemed to blend with the bleak landscape – a squat imitation of the slender monolith on the moor behind him. His clumsy fingers, curled round the shaft of the shovel, twitched spasmodically as he blundered through the threads of his thoughts like a blunt shuttle and his lips quivered as the fabric formed words in his mind. He was thinking of the case under his bed and the key concealed in the toe of his shoe.

'Move the key,' he whispered, nodding his bald head. 'She will find it yet.'

127

Having decided to move the key to the calf-shed, he laid down the shovel and stepped into the trench, trying not to damage the narrow channel at the bottom. Working backwards waist-deep in the drain, he began to lay the short, orange pipes, placing a clod of grass over each junction. He enjoyed this part of the work. The tiles squeezed so neatly into the clay, gradually forming a long, red cord deep in the earth. When it was covered no one would see his handiwork. It would be a secret like the person inside him.

'Move the key,' he repeated to himself as he broke another clod.

The light was fading when he laid the last tile at the end of the drain. Anxious to finish the contract that night, he hurriedly scraped the loose earth taken from the trench back into place. When he had finished, beads of sweat glistened on his head and slid down his temples. The overalls under his waterproof leggings were soaked with perspiration. He gathered his spades and shovels and stood them against the dyke. Then, hoisting on to his shoulder the huge, heart-shaped rutter with which he had opened the drain, he headed for home. The grass was already crisp with frost and a few faint stars had appeared behind the standing stone.

'Love is a dangerous word,' whispered the minister, scorching the timid souls in the pews beneath him with his angry glare until, under its withering beam, they melted into a malleable mass prepared for salvation.

'True love means obedience,' he continued quietly. 'Obedience to God and obedience to His laws. It means submission – submission to His will and to His word as spoken by His son and the prophets of old. It means a bowed head and a contrite heart.'

Again he paused to search the sea of eyes for signs of cynicism or blinks of indifference.

'It is not,' he roared suddenly, banging the pulpit, 'self-indulgence. Love does not need to wear scent, expose its flesh or paint its face. That is the way of the harlot. That leads to lust.'

His grey, curly hair, sprouting wildly from his head like bed-springs, shook violently as he spat out the last word. Frantically he searched the pews for a target, finally focussing on the round-faced youth in the third row whose gaze had strayed to the window.

'Lust,' he snarled, pointing his finger at the boy, 'is a poison which burns the bowels, a canker which consumes the heart, an evil which erodes the spirit. It is a fiery river flowing faster and faster into the tunnel of damnation.'

The startled youth below him trembled under the tirade, for he had been remembering his sister's sprouting breasts and the dark triangle between her thighs. How did the minister know? How did he read his mind? They could reach inside his head, these people – his stern, cold father and the demented creature above him. He could not escape. He could not hide the fantasies which tormented him. He closed his eyes, clasped his hands under his chin and pretended to pray, grinding his teeth to shut out the minister's voice.

When Donald Alec reached home he met his mother returning from the byre. She raised the lamp to see who was approaching.

'Is that you, Donald Alec?'

He could see that she was angry. Her little squint eyes, like those of a crab, peered at him through the lamplight, searching the crevices of his shell for signs of guilt. She is ugly, he thought, an old crone with lips like the broken-mouthed ewe that hangs about the doors – her pet, an ugly creature too.

'You are late,' she announced irritably, lowering the lamp and shuffling off her rubber boots at the door.

'I had the laird's drains to finish.'

'It is the prayer meeting tonight.'

'I had not forgotten.'

He too kicked off his boots and climbed the steep stair in his socks to his small room in the coomb. Feeling his way in the dark, he sat on the bed. He was searching for matches to light the lamp when she called up the stairway.

'Your tea is on the table. I am away now.' He wanted to
say 'Good' but he remained silent, waiting for the crunch of
her shoes on the gravel.

'And do not be smoking in your bedroom,' she shouted just
as he reached into the drawer for his cigarettes.

'Damn her!' he whispered angrily. 'How does she know
these things?'

Then he smiled, remembering that there were things that
she did not know. He was looking forward to his evening
alone.

The young man stood in the doorway, transfixed. He had
never seen a naked female till that moment. She was standing
in the zinc bath, gazing at the glowing embers in the grate,
unaware of his presence. Drops of water, glistening in the
lamplight, slid down her back and followed the curve of her
slim hips. He wanted to place his hands in the hollow of her
waist and feel the smooth flesh beneath his fingers but he
stood still, knowing that the whole scene would dissolve if she
heard him move. He was sure that she would soon hear the
thud of his heart and his quivering inhalations.

She turned to face him so quickly that he had no time to
retreat. She was shocked by his presence at first, and covered
her small breasts with her hands, but her alarm dissolved
quickly as she noticed the effect of her nakedness. She lowered
her hands and watched his eyes travel timidly round her
breasts. She sensed his fear and saw it twitch in his fingers
and flicker in his eyes. But she watched it drown in the tide
of his longing. He stood in the shadows like a stricken bull,
his open mouth oozing a string of saliva.

He wanted to move forward and enfold the gleaming flesh
in his wings. He wanted to enclose her in his mouth and hold
her in the hollow of his skull like a warm pearl. He wanted to
devour her lips, her breasts, her shoulders and her thighs but
he could not move.

Suddenly the vision shattered into sharp splinters of blinding light and a sickening pain shot through his head. He
stumbled against the wall, his legs folding beneath him.

'What kind of beast are you?' bellowed his father. 'Spying on the girl!'

Twice the big man kicked him in the thigh.

'Get out! Get out before I break every bone in your body!'

The boy crawled past him. As he staggered to his feet in the hall, he glanced back at his father. He could not understand the vicious punishment but he was sure that there was something more than censure in his father's eyes. He had seen the same expression when he had stolen his tobacco.

Donald Alec lifted the battered case on to the bed, unlocked it and stood back to admire the contents. He remembered how he had obtained the clothes. When his sister had married a Catholic in Glasgow, his father had cleared her room and bundled her belongings into a box.

'Burn these,' he had ordered, 'And see that every thread is consumed in the flames. She will not be back.'

But he had not burned them. When he shook out the contents he had found brilliantly coloured skirts and dresses, nylon stockings, high-heeled shoes, negligees and some underwear. As he handled the soft, scented garments they reminded him of his mother's clothes which he had worn occasionally as a child when left alone in the house. He had remembered the feeling of the smooth fabric on his skin and the comfort it had given. He had found some old clothes of his own and burned them instead. His sister's garments he had kept in the case.

He carried his mother's long mirror through from her bedroom and lit another lamp. Then he undressed and, standing in front of the glass, slipped into his sister's clothes.

He was excited and his thick fingers trembled as they fought with the tiny buttons. He enjoyed not only the feeling of the soft underclothes and the way they slid so easily across his skin, but also the freedom the clothes gave him to move around the house as a different person. When he was dressed he lifted his most precious possession from the case – a blonde wig. Combing it carefully into shape, he fitted it over his bald head and looked in the mirror. With his chest padded and his hips concealed in the loose dress he might have passed for a woman. He flounced away from the mirror and stepped carefully down the stairs, touching the rail delicately with two fingers.

The body lay in the head-rig against the dyke, its face the same colour as the grey granite boulders behind it. The right hand still clutched some of the seed corn. A few grains were embedded in the mud on his boots but the rest lay in a heap across his chest, spilled from the tilted sowing sheet. Three threadbare crows had spotted the carcass and were hopping over the legs, leaving a slob of crow shit like semen on the fly. They flew off resentfully as the son approached and perched on the standing stone, feigning disinterest. The young man stood over his father for some time, studying the thin blue lips. They would not snarl at him again. He kicked the sole of the old man's boot and turned away, leaving the eyes staring blindly at the blue sky.

As he passed the stackyard an immense yellow butterfly, just emerged from its chrysalis, fluttered unsteadily over the dyke. He had never seen one like it – its wings were almost as large as his hands – but, as he watched, it flitted too close to the ground and was caught by a hen. Within seconds the other birds gathered round and tore it to shreds. Unable to prevent its destruction, he stood helplessly in the yard, overwhelmed by anger, grief and loneliness.

Donald Alec sat with his legs crossed, admiring the sheen of the nylons and the elegance of the black shoes. As he lifted the porcelain teacup with his thumb and index finger, he felt like a woman. He felt warm and soft and full of giving, like a ripe udder. Yet he was not fulfilled. He longed to share his pleasure but, when he tried to think of someone with whom he could trust his secret, everyone had to be discounted. He did not like the men – they were harsh and unpredictable like his father – and he was afraid of women. He suspected that they could detect his frailty and he could not ascertain their response to it. If he confessed, they might turn on him and, like gulls over fish offal, pick him to pieces. On the other hand, they might laugh and ridicule and forgive. He wanted to know what they would say.

He replaced his cup and returned to his room to stand in front of the mirror. His mother would be returning soon. He would have to remove the clothes. He started to hoist the wig from his head but the caress of the long hair on his bare neck was so delightful that he let it fall back. He shook his head slowly so that the tresses touched his shoulders and watched the golden mane swing across his face in the mirror. He was a woman. He closed his eyes and ran his rough fingers down the flimsy dress, imagining female curves and folds beneath it. Once again he remembered his mother's return but could not bring the euphoria to an end. It was like flying. He was free to skim through the sky like a tern, wheeling, soaring, skimming over the sea. To step back into his other clothes would be like entering a prison. It would be cold and dark and lonely in there. He hated his other role. Why, then, should he play it? He stood still and stared at the mirror.

'Why should I?' he whispered.

Repeating this defiantly several times, he decided suddenly not to change his clothes.

Sitting in front of the mirror, he applied his sister's make-up to his face, clearly recalling her technique. He was pleased with the result when he had finished. His eyes seemed to shine from the mascara and his mouth, smeared with lipstick, was remarkably feminine. The transformation was so impressive that he decided to test it in the village.

The crowd in the inn was silent. Every face expressed a different emotion. Horror, confusion, disgust, amazement, amusement, sympathy, sorrow and dread could be seen in the dim light. The grotesque figure at the bar remained calm and detached, enveloped in a capsule of serenity. With his scarlet lips curved in a smile Donald Alec paid his debts, closed his handbag and left. In spite of the blue dress and blonde wig everyone recognised Donald Alec and, because they knew him so well, they realised that he was serious. They remained silent for a long time after his departure.

Donald Alec walked along the street, his high heels clicking on the pavement. He was at peace for the first time in many years. He watched the light on the reef blinking steadfastly in the Sound and the street lights rippling in the harbour. Gulls wheeled into the halo of light above the street and disappeared again into the night. He passed a group of young men sharing a can in a doorway.

'It's a bloody poof!' one of them said, tossing the can into the gutter.

'Calum!' he shouted towards another group ahead. 'Look at this! A real poof!'

Donald Alec continued his circuit of the streets, never thinking that the insults were directed at him. Even when the boys fell in behind him, making lewd suggestions, he was unaware of their hostility. It did not occur to him that he could come to harm in his own village. He was sailing in the calm seas of his own freedom, feeling the long hair move across his face as he walked and the soft dress slide across his knees.

When the boys ahead did not move out of his way, he stepped into the street to avoid them but they left the pavement and blocked his way. He did not realise their intentions till he was pushed. Then he saw the malice in their eyes. They encircled him like dogs round a rabbit and pushed him from one side of the ring to the other, chanting 'Poofter! Poofter!'

As he staggered across the street, his wig fell off and they kicked it into the sea.

He did not resist or plead with them to stop but allowed himself to be tossed about. He was a woman. He remembered his mother gasping for breath when his father flung her against the wall. This was the cost of being a woman – humiliation, degradation, subjugation. The more he submitted, the more viciously he was attacked.

They left him in the roadway, his bald head black with mud, his torn skirt round his waist, his high heels broken and his lipstick smeared with blood.

DOG-ENDS

G. M. McFadden

It was no joke, no joke at all. Here in the park in his slept-in
clothes reduced to this, picking up dog-ends with the sun up
there bright and hot making the five-day shirt stick to his body
and everybody watching him – fucksake – had they nothing
better to do? All lying there healthy and shining and trying
to get brown all over; funny, he'd been like that once a lot of
summers ago with the girl-friends and the sun-tan lotion and
the cans of Coke and the cheese pieces and the white cold
dollops of ice-cream.

But dreaming was no use. Dreaming wouldn't help the
here-and-now, the hunger and having no fags and needing a
curer after all the drink the day before, too much fucking drink
on an empty stomach as well. Turns you into a scarecrow, so
it does – thin as a stick, a fucking matchstick man! – you can't
go on like that and just go on and on, the same carry-on every
Thursday, throwing the giro all over the place one day and
wakening up with fuck-all the next.

He stooped to kid on he was tying his shoelace and picked
up the dog-end he'd spotted – half a fag at least, a bit squashed
under the heel but a prize all the same – and he wandered on,
looking for more dog-ends and maybe some empty lemonade
bottles and maybe even the odd coin that might have been
dropped somewhere like manna from heaven.

Christ, this heat, it was too much; he must be stinking with
all the sweat, and he couldn't get a bath to wash it off, he
hadn't even had a shave for three days. He came to the fountain with the gargoyles spewing water from the stone mouths
and the tiny splashes splintering in the sun-bright water pool,
and he sat on a bench where he'd spotted some dog-ends and
shredded and rolled the one he'd found and lit it, watching

the weans splashing around in the water and throwing wet
handfuls of it all over each other, and the people – the summer
people – sprawled here and there on the grass, trying to get
brown because they thought brown was a nicer colour to be,
drinking their Cokes and lemonade and chatting and giggling
and bantering and some of them watching him picking up the
dog-ends around the bench with long quick fingers.

He was past caring, he really was. It was all bad enough
anyway without being watched as well, as if he was on a stage
with his humiliation and the park was the theatre and the
summer people were the audience. He preferred the park in
winter when there were no people and he could get peace, and
he'd feel a bit better because all of it – the bare trees, branches
like old men's arms, and the dying green of the ups-and-downs
and the unturning roundabouts and unswinging swings – it
felt like it was all his, there was a sort of hollowness echoing
back a childhood countryside a long distance of memory ago
full of quiet hills and slow roads all in a dusty haze and no
endless streets and traffic racket and crowd chatter – all the
city thunder and forevermotion – to freeze all the feeling out
of him.

A bastard, so it was, but he couldn't seem to get away from
it – not really away – he could only get away from it a wee
bit in the park, but staying in the park forever just wasn't on.
He'd have to go home sometime, home – for fuck's sake! –
home to the squat with the rats and the mingled stench of the
damp and the pish and the shit and the scrap of carpet and
the wee stump of candle that was all that was left before he'd
need cat's eyes to see at night.

It would get on your wick, the whole thing! Ha, ha, ha; but
you had to laugh sometimes because if you didn't you'd go
mad with all this living like that, the living that made you do
all this putting off the going home to climb in the window and
light the candle and feed the rats and the poor wee ferret as
long as there was something left over from the scraps he'd
picked up in the morning from outside the shops, the fruit and
vegetables and things that were meant not to be eaten.

It was no joke, but you got used to it over the years like

you get used to most things; and it even had something going
for it, he supposed, like not having to get caught up in all that
fucking madness out there – all the helter-skelter and never a
minute to spare – it was too much for him, he couldn't take
all that, it knotted his gut and screwed him up and got him
drinking too much which only made things worse in the end
when it all came down to it, with his pockets empty and –

'Excuse me, have you a light?'

A woman's voice, very polite. She'd stopped by the bench
with the cigarette held between her lips, face bright with sun,
eyes squinting the question down at him, and as he took the
box of matches from his pocket, she leant towards him, pushing hair back from her face, and he lit the cigarette and
decided to chance it because she looked well-off, she'd probably just forgotten to bring her lighter with her.

'Could you do me a favour?'

She must have guessed what the favour was going to be,
because her fingers were already fumbling with the clasp on
her handbag and she was taking out the purse and opening it
while he was telling her he was short of twenty pence for his
bus fare and it was a real problem because he had a sick
mother and he needed to see her right away. She poked around
in the purse, then her fingers came back out holding four shiny
tenpees, and she dropped them into his hand.

'You look hungry.'

'Aye. I'm starving.'

'You'll get something to eat?'

'I'll get something.'

And that was that. She went away to meet whoever it was
she was going to meet, and he was left there alone again with
his brand new tenpees, his whole forty pee, wondering what
he could spend it all on while the weans went on splashing in
the fountain and the summer people went on getting brown
and laughing and talking and all that carry-on and an ice-
cream van tinkled a funny wee tune into the middle of it all.

He was going to pick up the rest of the dog-ends around
the bench when he decided not to bother; it seemed a bit daft
to do that when he'd the forty pee and he could buy four

singles, four whole fags. It was embarrassing, but he was past caring about doing things like that – you got thick-skinned over the years – going into shops and buying singles and advertising to every cunt that he didn't have a tosser!

It was better than picking up the dog-ends though – anything was better than that – so he left the ones he was going to pick up and raised himself from the bench and started walking again back the way he'd come, feet moving faster this time, the four tenpees jangling together in his pocket and the four singles doing a wee jig before his eyes, past the trees then the ice-cream van and the queue of the summer people all sweaty and bare-limbed and rolled in sun-gold, mouths slack and gasping fish-like for the cold sweet slither in the throat that would make them enjoy even more their break from the ever-turning roundabout with its whirling blur of crowds and streets and buildings and the trying to have more than each other and the wanting more and more and the not being able to jump off the roundabout, forever anyway – not forever – maybe just for the odd days, days like today with the sun shining.

It was no joke for them either, it really couldn't be very funny, but they'd probably got used to living like that, in the helter-skelter most of the week and in the park at the weekends when the sun came out, just like he'd got used to living the way he did and always with fuck-all or the next thing to it like the four tenpees and the dancing singles. It was funny though – it really was – watching them the same way they'd watched him with the five-day shirt and the picking up dog-ends, it was funny watching them in their artificial countryside all happy with their sun and their weans and their ice-cream, and why not! Fucksake, why not! They'd the park for a day, that was all, they'd never find a foreverpark, poor bastards; it was no joke for them, no joke at all.

DARKNESS MADE VISIBLE
Susan Chaney

Rain hit the windscreen in an oily yellow arc and leaf skeletons came swirling from the darkness. The air tasted cold: a tingling November coldness. The beginning of winter. Frost on the lawn and fireworks and beyond the house the young moon floating in a shawl of cloud. But the house was far behind us now. We had been driving for a long time. At first I had traced our progress across the map with my fingers. It had pleased me for a while. Cornwall was pink, Devon eggshell blue and Somerset green. But now my head was beginning to ache and the backs of my legs were sticking damply to the seat. I turned to the window but all I could see was my own reflection. It had been too dark to see the white horse carved out of the chalk when we crossed Salisbury Plain. I was sad. The white horse was a friend of mine. A landmark. Someone I could rely on.

The car took a corner too sharply and I slid across the leather seat. I grabbed for the hanging strap but missed and my head banged listlessly against the glass. Books, dolls, comics and puzzles thudded to the floor. My mother didn't turn round.

It was raining harder now and the back of the car was cavernous and damp. The windows were clouded with condensation. Little trickles of moisture were spilling from the frames and collecting around the tarnished metal handle that wound the windows down. Every so often a large drop would form on the underside and fall with a dull plopping sound onto the rubber matting. Everything felt mouldy. Once I'd found an ants' nest in the crumbling upholstery. It was an old, heavy car. An Armstrong Siddeley built just after the War. It had curved wooden running boards and enormous domed headlights which my father polished lovingly every Sunday morning. He kept it fanatically clean, spending hours with Duraglit, chamois leather and wax.

'A perfect excuse for him to keep himself out of the house,' my mother would say, with *that* look on her face. The look she reserved just for him: her eyes narrowed, her mouth pulled down. Cruel but powerless. I didn't like my mother when she looked like that.

I hated that car and I hated him for buying it. I knew it was only because he'd got it cheap: because no one else had wanted it. Being seen with him in that car caused me agonies of embarrassment. Why couldn't we have a normal car? Like other people. Something ordinary. Something discreet. A Mini perhaps? Or a Cortina.

We were driving down an avenue of trees – the headlights picking out banks of leaves and dripping foliage. As we swung around a bend in the road the tree trunks appeared to be rushing towards us; each one momentarily illuminated, for a split second fantastically alive and then dropping back into the blackness. Like embers. Extinguished.

An overhanging branch lashed against the windscreen. The car swerved and my father swore. It teetered out across the road, the wheels spinning on the wet surface. It shuddered violently but he managed to hold it. He held it but only just. It had been close. I was frightened. So was he. *And* he knew that he'd been wrong, that he'd been too close to the edge. I could tell by the way he glanced across at my mother: sheepish but belligerent. Steeling himself for the onslaught yet determined to defend himself; to deny everything. But my mother said nothing. She just sat there, staring ahead. Saying nothing.

Darkness and rain. My father leaning forwards gripping the wheel. One hand moving across the dashboard, turning the knob that worked the windscreen wipers. Turning them back and forth, grunting slightly with the effort. My father's hand tightening and slackening, the veins bulging blue and livid in the artificial light.

Darkness and rain. My mother sitting there beside him, so

small, so quiet. So small she was that I could only just see the top of her head poking up from the looming back of her seat. So small she was that from the outside even when she wore her big furry Russian hat and sat on two cushions she could barely be seen. All the children laughed at her. I had known for a long time that she was absurd and yet, as the miles passed, I felt a growing awe of her as she sat there wrapped in her silence.

A car approached and we dipped our lights. As they dazzled out again the raindrops danced in a blur of gold.

'We are making darkness visible,' I said to myself because I knew nothing.

All I understood was that we were travelling through the darkness towards an unknown hospital where a demented old lady rocked in her bed. Somewhere in the darkness she bent forwards: skinny in her stained nightie, brandishing an imaginary whip and shouting, 'Home, James and don't spare the horses.'

The day the telegram came, the storm had finally blown itself out after battering the coast for several days. Boats had been lost and the sea front at Penzance had been smashed by twenty-foot waves. Everyone said it was the worst storm for fifty years. We had stayed inside watching it on the news. But now the sea and sky were glassy with the thin blue transparency that comes in the wake of a storm. On the horizon there was only a fine, tumbled ribbon of cloud. Everywhere was that trembling light, that feeling of expansion, of mysteries about to reveal themselves. A light wind was blowing, laced with the beginning of real cold. The blood was singing in my finger-tips as I raced across the beach.

Masses of seaweed lay shining and tangled on the sand. The air was thick with the smells of salt, oil and splintered wood. The red clay, gouged from the cliffs by the sea, lay in heaps, startling against the white granite rocks. Rust-coloured rivulets trickled down towards the sea. In one place a section of fencing sagged dangerously over the cliff, the twisted wire and broken posts jutting raggedly into the sky. The corpses of jellyfish and starfish were strewn everywhere – the tiny suckers on their fingers contracted like so many disapproving mouths.

I found a whole crate of oranges and a bottle of French wine in a straw basket.

I saw them all through the window before I went back into the house. They were all together in the front room; my mother, my father and my two sisters. I was surprised to see them like that. Usually we only met at meal times. Quietly I laid the crate of oranges down. A trail of slimy juice oozed out and dribbled down onto the step. As I opened the door the room closed around me. It smelt of stale cigarette smoke and paraffin and the sad, dusty scent of worn upholstery. All the chairs were frayed: the white paintwork was stained a drab yellow.

My mother was sitting; my sisters Viv and Evie and my father standing together, apart from her. My father held the telegram in one hand: his folded paper clasped under the other arm. He must have been the one who opened it.

Turning to the mirror my eldest sister deftly traced her mouth with a dull pink lipstick. I knew its real name was Ashes of Roses but Evie and I preferred to call it Shit Pink. I didn't think it suited her, it made her mouth look too pale and grudging. Shutting the lipstick with a decisive little click, appearing to take charge of the situation, she said to my father, 'Couldn't she go on the train?'

He didn't answer and she shrugged. 'Anyway, whatever happens *I'm* not coming. I'm far too busy studying for my prelims just now.'

I could see that he was struggling: he didn't think quickly. For a moment his mouth looked vulnerable and I wanted to touch him, but then his thin lips tightened into a more familiar expression. As he regained control his brown eyes blanked over.

'No,' he said, 'I'll drive her. You know what she's like. She'd never manage to cross London on her own. You can stay here with Evie and we'll take Hilary with us.'

Crossing to my mother's chair I stood uncertain beside her. She looked up at me and my stomach turned. Her face wore

its other look: the look that turned me inside out with pain.
The fine skin across her cheekbones was stretched to transparency and all the blue had gone from her eyes.

'It's Granny,' Evie piped up, cocky with self-importance,
sure of herself again, now that she knew she was spared.

'She's been taken into hospital. It's senile dementia.'

She spoke the two words slowly and carefully, savouring
them. Lowering her voice, she whispered dramatically, 'That
means she's gone batty.'

I glanced guiltily at my mother, knowing that later on when
we were in bed Evie would supply the details, real or imagined, and we would laugh together about it.

My father shifted the gears and looked at his watch, grunting
with satisfaction.

'Not bad. Not bad,' he muttered. 'We should be on the
outskirts of Reading soon. From there we'll get a clear run on
to Cambridge.'

The plan was we would stay the night with his mother in
Cambridge and then drive over to the hospital the next day.

'That way,' Viv and Evie had explained to me, 'he's saving
himself the cost of an hotel and getting to visit his own mother,
which he hasn't done in ages.'

I looked at the back of his head. His thin grey hair was
sleeked down with Brylcreem and a few wiry hairs straggled
from his ears. Was he really that bad? I didn't like to think
so. After all he was my father and I loved him, didn't I? Evie
and Viv claimed they couldn't stand the sight of him: that he
was a selfish, tightfisted, bad-tempered old so and so. But that
was because he banged on the bathroom door in the mornings
making them come out before they'd finished washing and he
wouldn't pay for them to go to the pictures on a Friday night.
And yet? And yet? How *come* all the other girls at school had
five shillings a week pocket money and I only got half-
a-crown?

Cambridge Granny's flat smelt of gas and reminded me of the
War. In one corner stood a large old-fashioned radio. The

windows were draped with heavy lace curtains. The wallpaper was a pale sepia shade with the paintwork picked out in dark brown. 'Nigger brown,' she called it. There were lots of brass and photographs in heavy frames and things called anti-macassars on the backs of the chairs.

She crept forwards to greet us, a massive old woman dressed in black with thick lisle stockings and a double rope of pearls strung beneath her sagging throat. Her fine white hair was scraped so tightly across her head that I could see her pale pink scalp. It reminded me of a mouse's tail. She was holding her body as if in pain, with one hand clasped to her hip, but her eyes were clear and bright and her cheeks were flushed a healthy pink. She glared at my mother.

'Well, I must say, Agnes, you certainly know how to pick your time, don't you? It couldn't be worse. Couldn't be worse.'

Her tone implied that only a very inferior kind of person could be that inconsiderate. Turning to my father, she allowed her lips to tremble slightly.

'My arthritis is very bad just now, George, and my chest has been troubling me again lately. The doctor says I shouldn't have any excitement. That I should take things easy.'

Painstakingly drawing herself up as though falling back upon years of breeding, she said, 'But I'm forgetting myself. I'm alone too much, I'm becoming a selfish old woman. *Dear* Agnes. Sit yourself down. You must be tired after your journey.' Holding my mother at arm's length, looking her slowly up and down. 'What a pretty hat you're wearing, dear. It takes years off her, don't you think so, George?'

My mother sank into a chair and I crossed to the window overlooking the river. Turning back I stared at the adults in the room. Were these people *really* my parents? My grandmother? As I swung back to the window my breath clouded the pane. I wrote 'HELP' in big, shaky letters, quickly dragging my sleeve through it before they could read it.

The rain had cleared and a fresh little breeze had sprung up. The water lapped at the far bank with a tense, hollow sound. Closing my eyes, I leaned against the glass. For a moment I thought I was at home by the sea listening to the waves sucking back from the shore. When I opened them again I saw three students cycling past. They were wearing brightly coloured woollen hats and their long college scarves were blowing behind them. In the clear air their voices sounded pure and high. They were innocent and I was not.

'Take me with you,' I cried silently into the cold glass. 'Please, I don't care who you are or where you're going, just take me with you.'

The next morning my mother looked grey and tired as if she hadn't slept at all. She was dressed and ready by eight o'clock – standing by the window checking and rechecking her purse and her gloves, straightening her stockings repeatedly.

'Oh, do sit down, can't you Agnes?' snapped Granny from the breakfast table. 'You're giving me the willies, you really are. And anyway,' she continued, slowly, deliberately buttering a piece of toast, 'I shan't be ready for at least another hour.'

'*You?*'

'Yes, I'm coming for the drive. George agrees with me that I don't get out enough, and a run in the car would be good for me.'

Nine o'clock and my father was finally washed and shaved. Granny was standing in front of the mirror securing her hat with pins. They were very old-fashioned: steel-blue, long, elegant and very sharp, with carved mother-of-pearl on the ends. As she stabbed them through the taut fabric they made a slight ripping noise. Her heavy old face was puce with satisfaction.

My mother spoke. 'Surely you're not going in that old sweater, George?'

He sighed. 'Of course not. I'll change it as soon as I've cleaned the car.'

Her face was very still and when she spoke it was as if the words were being dragged from somewhere deep inside of her. Some part of her I had never seen before.

'But, George, what about my mother? It always takes you ages to clean that car. I'll barely have any time at all with her.'

His face closed like a trap.

'Look,' he said with exaggerated patience, as though explaining something for the umpteenth time to a slow child. 'You know how I feel. I simply won't drive through Cambridge in a dirty car. And anyway, does it really make that much difference? She won't know you. You realise that, don't you?'

I knew what Viv and Evie would have said to her. I could hear them clearly as if they were in the room with us.

'Kick him in the balls. Take his money,' they would have said to my mother. 'Catch a bus. A train. Hitch a lift. Fight. Run. Anything. Just do something. Just get out of there.'

But it was different for them. I didn't have their certainty, their clarity of purpose. Besides they were older than me. They were old enough to be left alone, to have boyfriends. Soon they would be old enough to leave altogether. And anyway I could see now something that they didn't know. That it was too late. That it had been too late for a long time.

It was cold outside as we stood together watching him clean the car. His hands were blue: the knuckles looking raw and swollen. As he raised the dripping sponge they steamed in the brittle air.

The car was a pale, dappled green with exactly the same marbled texture as an unripened apple. As he slowly drew the cloth over the smooth surface I could feel the bitter saliva scouring the insides of my cheeks and rushing into my mouth. The chrome headlights were clouded with polish. As he rubbed at them in fussy, circular motions the metal began to gleam and I saw my mother's face hanging there, reflected. As he drew the cloth again and again across her image it kept distorting and then reforming. Upside down, inside out, now shrunken, now elongated. Always with the same expression, those eyes floating helpless.

I knew I was looking at darkness. Darkness made visible.

THE MAP OF AUSTRALIA
Rosalind Brackenbury

'Terra Australis Non Dum Cognita'. Abraham Ortelius, 1587.

On the map of existence made at that time, there is a line which goes clear and exact for a few inches, then wavers, and then stops. It is like a crust. What goes on beneath it has to be guessed at. The earliest explorers, the Dutch, sailed these coastlines and drew their careful charts. They were honest. They did not pretend to know more than they did. They did not sketch anything in until they were sure. There were these great gaps, where storms arose and the coastline became invisible and they were swept out to sea, battered by weather, and lost their bearings. They left the gaps. The gaps are there on the old maps, in the museum, and they take your breath away, they are as alarming as gaps on a temperature chart or an electrocardiograph, they are simply places where everything has to stop, everything founders. But we are used to continuity and everything being filled in. We are more alarmed than they were.

'This is Katherine, she lives in Australia
With her parents, her pets and her paraphernalia.'

He laughed at paraphernalia. He knew what it was, now. And the way that fascinating word got into the story at all.

– You don't have much paraphernalia, do you, Markie? He had a wooden house stuffed with toys from the disposal store and other children's houses, and a small cardboard suitcase with his clown suit in it, and a wand to balance plates on for his act. He had a hat, which made motherly middle-aged women drop tears. He had a fleet of battered, wheel-less metal cars.

– Again. Read again.

– Not *again*. I do think we'll have to get you a new book.
Pity we've missed *Sesame Street*. Look, why don't you play with
your cars?

– Read again. Par'phernalia.

– If it hadn't bloody well been Australia, we wouldn't have
had to have that word. What about Katherine who lives in
Tasmania?

– With the birds and the bees and her megalomania?

There was the engine sound, the truck rattling up over
stones, roaring to get over rocks in the road. Brakes, and
the silence afterwards. Markie ran, naked except for his
tee-shirt, buttocks still paler than the rest of him, twin
hard-boiled eggs' halves in the gloom of the house. He ran
into sunlight, between the flashing gums, into the marbled
outdoors. He loved the Ute and all that was mechanical.
He roared his engine sound, he was all trunk, screaming
his brakes to a halt. He ran towards Louis, who banged
the truck door hard and came towards him, not hurrying,
across the yards of light. The dog sprang out, jumped,
licked, nearly felled him. He became part man, part truck,
part dog. He was fluid, part of them all. Overhead, the sun
shot him in the small of the back, propelling him forward.
Louis smiled and swung him high. He did not know who
this man was, but was part of him. He was Louis, as the
dog was the dog, and the Ute was the Ute, and he was
Markie, and the word, paraphernalia, Australia, whatever
it was, linked them all like a long chain, an inevitability
running through this moment and the whole of his life.

The thin line of the map of Markie's experience wavered in
some places and left gaps so that sometimes he could not
remember what was where and how it had been. Mostly the
gaps did not bother him, for what was all around him now
was his and all to hand; he could reach out for it as he had
for his mother when he wanted her breast and as he did now
for his toy cars and dumper trucks. He could look up, look
around him and see that there were not any gaps in evidence;

the floor went on quite smoothly all around him, there were noises within earshot, the noise of the Ute's engine coming up the hill was one he knew, and the light thump-thump was the dog scratching at her fleas. He could sit in the middle of his world and watch it spread around him, sunlight making patterns on the floor, dust in the air, trees outside, blue sky beyond trees. He could shout and hear his own voice. There was his mother, who refused him her breast now, tucking it out of sight beneath her tee-shirt, but who would usually give him something, a finger of bread, a cup with milk in it, a cuddle, a word. She was the link with all the rest, the things he was forgetting. She and the battered suitcase with the clown things in it. He knew that the battered suitcase had been somewhere else, in that place that now had no outline and no solidity. And the clown things. They, like him, had come from somewhere else. There was his hat and his stick and the plate he balanced and some clothes now that were tight on him when she tried them on. He struggled, pulled at them, tore some threadbare material, heard her crossness.

– Oh, Markie, look, now I'll have to mend it. What a nuisance. Now, take those off carefully, will you?

He was quite grave and passive, let her take the clothes off him. It was clear to both of them that they would very soon be too small to go on at all. And at the same time he was not allowed to tug at her freckled breasts, not wanted there any more, was even pushed quite roughly away. The feeling of that too, of sucking, of knowing that firm outline quite clearly through his clutching hands, that was going. Milk in a cup was quite different. It was silly to call them the same word. Milk, he said clearly, and all that it had ever meant in his life of closeness, of warmth, of her, was gone. It was cold stuff in cold plastic. He tipped it on the floor, made a small white puddle. He pretended not to hear. Words lied. Milk was the experience he was losing, forgetting. He began to pretend that he could not speak at all.

Louis said – You'll have to be firm. Don't give in to him. He should have been weaned long ago.

He hated Louis. He pummelled him with his fists. Louis

was the man he wanted to be, the man with the Ute and the shovel, but he also hated him for the sound of his voice when he spoke those words, for the way he sat next to his mother on the sofa watching TV, for the way he looked. Markie picked up a bowl from the table because of the feeling and threw it on the floor. It had the remains of Louis's soup in it.

– Markie. Louis' voice had a hard edge like the table when you banged your head. It did not sound like Louis but like someone else. Who? Markie wondered if somebody else was inside Louis, a man with a voice like that, hard-edged.

His mother said to Louis – God, whoever spoke to you like that: You'll scare him out of his wits.

Louis said – He has to learn.

The soup and the bowl stayed on the floor. The face stayed on the television, pink and talking. The dog came peacefully and licked up all the soup and Markie's milk as if she were the only one of them all who could do anything. Louis held his mother on the sofa, either with a hand or with his voice. The words hung about the room – He has to learn. The room seemed dangerous all at once. Markie wanted his mother to move and for things to be ordinary again, but they were not.

It was like the business with the potty. He knew what to do in the potty but was sometimes elsewhere when it happened to him, the sudden pleasure of it pushing its way out of his body. Then, he picked it up carefully from wherever it fell and carried it into the house across the floor and dropped it into the potty. Then he would wait for one of them to be pleased. When the dog did it he carried it for her too. Long brown sausages smelling different to his. He made the collection, put it all in the same place. His mother laughed.

Louis said – He's playing with dog shit again.

– I don't think he realises it's any different to his.

– He'll have to learn. It can't be hygienic, picking it up in his fingers like that.

– Hygienic! D'you think having the dog eat off his plate's hygienic? Or living with flies all over the place? Markie, go and wash your hands. You're not to touch Cleo's shit any more.

There were all these complications in life.

He trotted to the bathroom.

Louis said – D'you want to have a shower with me? I'm having a shower. Things became quieter inside him. Louis in the shower was dark brown, the colour of wood with white patches. He had patches of hair and a penis that looked alive. He ducked his head under the shower of water and with water streaming down his face and through his beard he looked like some of the trees in the rain forest, all shaggy and wet.

Suddenly Markie remembered that there had been another man, a different colour but doing the same thing, sluicing himself with water and then turning the trickle on to Markie himself. He felt the water, and hands washing him. Heard his mother's voice some way away. The feeling went with being cold, and the colour was different, the colour of it all was different; and then there was a soft furry feeling under his feet and he was being wrapped up and rubbed in front of a staring hot thing that was red and would burn him if he touched. The line of that bit of his experience existed, stretched, wavered, gave way to nothing else. It was simply there. It was simply somewhere else.

There was also somewhere a line of bars. He was being carried past them upward. What waited was the sky, and wetness. He was close to his mother, perhaps still part of her. The wetness touched his face and hands. The bars receded, but not until they had shut out part of the sky. His mother told him that they had come from somewhere else. – Don't you remember, coming in the aeroplane, coming across the sea? It wasn't very long ago. Don't you remember? And Louis coming to meet us at the airport.

He knew they had been in an aeroplane for a long time; but also that he had been asleep for most of it. Now, when he saw an aeroplane in the sky there was no connection. It was like hearing that in another existence he had been a bird. And now that Louis was here, part of his every day, he could not remember a time of meeting him. There was a time before, and then there was now which was reality, in which he and his mother and Louis and Cleo the dog all lived. Sometimes his mother told him about the other place which was called London, but it was like hearing something he did not need, like being given too much to eat. When she showed him books with pictures of what she called England, he did not want to look. He preferred the ones about Australia, which was where he lived and was real. 'This is Katherine, she lives in Australia.' It gave him a warm sense, almost as if she lived with them. In the story she went on a journey from where she lived in the bush to a place called Sydney where there was a lot of traffic and noise. Of course she liked her home in the bush best, and went back to it at the end of the story, to her horse and her mummy and daddy and brothers and sisters. He thought of going away from here and never coming back and it made him shiver inside. He decided that he would never, ever go away. If you left a place even for a while, it might stop being there. It might go thin and be hard to remember and have no lines to contain it. He could not take the risk that Katherine had, not even for a day.

His mother told him that soon he would be going to a creche in Launceston where he would stay while she did some work. He screamed and lay on the floor and pretended again that he could not speak, so that she would know he was a baby and so could not go. He peed on the floor in a pool and went to eat some of Cleo's food out of her bowl. If he was a dog they would not send him anywhere.

Louis said – I think he's a bit too young.

His mother said – Well, if you won't look after him. What else can I do?

– He can stay with me. If it's only for a few days. And his mother said nothing, unfamiliarly. The silence afterwards was as if several people were talking, only you could not hear what they had to say.

*

He played in his house over and over again, the same game. The house was one that Louis had found in a disposal shop and had repaired for him. It had a roof that took off so that you could get inside squashed up between the four walls and pull down the roof over your head. With his knees up over his nose he sat in there. Outside the house were all his toys, the sagging teddies, the worn and faceless dolls, the metal cars with most of the paint bashed off. Most of his toys had belonged to other children, children he did not know. Inside the house there was just himself filling it up completely. And he played the game of somebody coming to visit him, of sitting there and waiting for them to come up to the outside of the house and knock and ask if he, Markie, were at home. He was not sure who the person was; sometimes it was one of the teddies or the dolls and sometimes it was somebody invisible. But it was somebody who had come from a long way away to find him. The person knocked and asked for food and a cup of tea. The person came in and was with him in the squashed space drinking tea. He poured cup after cup, talking all the while in the language he had that his mother and Louis did not understand. The person understood. The person was so close that he did not have to explain anything, and when the person went after all his cups of tea and slices of cake, Markie felt entirely satisfied. He played the game over and over again.

His mother said – He's very quiet all of a sudden. What d'you think he's doing in there?

Louis said – Makes a change. I guess they do get to an age where they play by themselves.

Markie said to the person in his house – Would you like another cup of tea?

When Louis went away in the Ute, Markie stood with his arm up against his eyes in the dazzle of sunlight. Cleo the dog ran and barked, leaving the old wallaby bone she was chewing, and leapt into the back as the truck moved off. Louis had forgotten to ask Markie if he wanted to go too. Markie shouted

and shouted, out there alone in the pools of light. He did not
want to be with his mother, who was smoking a cigarette and
reading, and he did not want to play his game. He only wanted
to be with Louis. Louis was going off to work on the land
without him, as if he did not exist. He stood and howled. The
whole morning, bright and glittery as it was, broke around
him in pieces that would never mend. Wanting to go was as
sharp as wanting to pee. He could do nothing against it. Wanting to be in the front with Louis, racketing away down the
hill, over the stones and through the creek, was the strongest
thing he had ever felt. Perhaps it would never go away and
never change.

His mother had told him – Louis is not your father.

Was it only fathers that wanted boys along with them? Was
that why Louis sometimes forgot?

Wanting, he screamed and peed. The dog raced up and
down in the back of the truck as Louis backed it, and barked
and barked. The Ute hit a stone and stalled. Louis got out
again, shifted the stone and saw him. The dog, with spit flying
from her mouth, leapt up and down. The whole thing had
stopped for him, could start again when Louis said. Markie
stopped screaming in case it put Louis off. He often said that
he couldn't stand whingeing kids.

– Want to come? Louis sounded as if it were easy just to
change everything.

– Well, get some shoes and put your pants on. Peed
yourself, have you? Ulla – he shouted in case she heard –
I'll take him along. She looked up from her cigarette and
book, relieved. She was pleased whenever she saw him and
Louis going away. But going away with Louis was safe,
would always be, because Louis would always come back,
this was Louis' only real place too, he had made it, he had
built it, his house.

Markie could not remember exactly when it was that he knew
she was not coming back.

The days went on one after another; he slept in the little
bed upstairs, just through the wall from where Louis slept. In

the morning he heard Louis thumping about, the rattle of the dog's claws on the wood floor, the voice of the man talking to the dog, the dog not answering but looking at him, Markie knew, as if she wanted to answer. He would wake with wanting to pee. Sometimes he peed the bed and Louis would shout at him, but not angrily, not like he used to, just loud and cross and then quite friendly again. More and more often he woke with the feeling but able to hold it until he was quite awake and go carefully down the ladder then holding on to his penis until he reached the bathroom. Sometimes there was Louis there holding his own big dark one like a snake and pissing his own stream into the bowl. Louis quite often peed outside, staring out between the gum trees as he did so. Markie copied him in everything he did; somehow with his mother not there it was easier to be like Louis. He felt like Louis, sometimes he was even sure he was him. He strode about, and swore. Like this he would be safe from being sent to the creche in Launceston, from being shut in somewhere where he would die. This was Louis' place and his. Nobody could move either of them any more.

The days were all very much the same. Louis burned the toast on the stove in the mornings as the logs flared and shifted inside. He made tea and drank it standing up, fished out the tea leaves with one finger and flicked them to the floor. He went for a shit and read a magazine in there and left the door a crack open. He came out and shouted at Markie to be ready, to put on his shoes. He was always shouting about shoes and would wallop him if he went outside without them, because of the snakes. They would both carry the breakfast things to the sink, Markie carrying his own milk mug, and there would be a stack of stuff toppling. Then they would go off together to start the Ute.

The morning would not be too hot, early. Now that his mother was not there nobody talked about the heat anyway and he could go without his hat because Louis never nagged about hats, only shoes. They went, the two of them. The Ute started; Louis backed it, hit a rock, swore, began again. The dog jumped into the back. Markie sat in front and held on. As they went away down the hill the rocks leapt up to meet them and crashed against the floor. The trees flew at them. The sky was cracked open by so many trees, rushed down into the gaps. At the corner the dog always leapt out to run alongside, barking. Louis stopped the truck in the same place. Today was like yesterday. He was clearing the land, rooting up the stumps of old gum trees, burning them. There were black warm stumps in weird shapes, smoking. Louis said he was going to plant vines. Markie believed him because Louis always did what he said, but he could not think how he would do it because of what his mother had once said – How the hell you're going to clear that lot and plant a vineyard, I can't imagine.

The borders of what his mother could imagine confined him; but he watched Louis with his pick split the stumps and heave them out of the earth. He watched them smoulder and the spaces between them grow. He took a small fork and struck the earth. It was too hard to dig. He sat down on the ground and watched ants spiralling out of a hole. He thought of her sitting outside the house with her cigarettes, waiting for something to happen; and then out on the terrace juggling, making that happen. Her hands controlled the little flying soft bags as they controlled everything. They pushed him away from her and then held him close. Louis said he should be weaned by now. The word, weaned, had a mean with-holding sound. When Louis had said that, he hated him. He thought, how would you like it. His own hands remembered still the shape and feel of her breast. His mouth sucked and wanted to bite. She pushed him away. A mug of cold milk was put in his hand. He spat the milk and the lying word that went with it. If that was called milk, then everything was something else, words did not do.

He was not a baby any more, maybe not even a boy. The only thing to be was a man. Or an ant. Louis was a man, you pushed at Louis and he simply went on working. To and fro, to and fro, as his mother had once said, like an ant. Louis never stopped until it was time to. He never did nothing all day, as his mother did. He worked then he stopped, looked at the sun, wiped a dirty hand across his forehead and said that it was time for lunch. Then they got back in the Ute and drove back up the rocky track. The sun was hitting them on the back of the head. The dog was running and panting. The rocks rose up again like walls. The house was a box of coolness, with flies. The flies feasted on the breakfast things. Louis cut cheese in long slices and made cheese on toast. The smell of burning and the burning of his fingers with dripping waxy cheese went together. They ate side by side on the settee, the table piled high with papers. Louis read as he ate and made a clicking noise as he chewed. Markie chewed and found it hard to swallow. He turned the mass of chewed up toast and cheese in his mouth and tried to make it go down. He wanted to spit. If he spat Louis would shout at him. Very quietly while Louis was reading, he crept to the dog's bowl and spat the revolting mass. He looked at it, brown and slimy, flecked with spit. The dog bit it up with a snap. Louis looked up, said nothing. Markie had a mouth full of spit and a wet chin. The dog still had hungry eyes but licked her lips. Markie wandered back to Louis, wanting something. Something was not there but also blocked his throat so that he could not swallow and could not speak. It was a day like all the others, just as hot and blue and dry and speechless, with these times in it when nothing at all moved.

Louis never said, as far as he could remember, that she was not coming back. Perhaps Louis himself did not know. Locked into a rhythm of activity and sleep, the two of them never asked each other, never said.

A few days, she had said. A workshop somewhere in town, a meeting of circus artistes in Hobart. Was it that neither of them had really listened when she said, or that neither had heard? Just while I set something up. The creche if you can't manage. Not long. Perhaps Louis, like Markie, had not really listened when she said it. Perhaps she was somewhere near, not far away at all but looking at them and listening to them, behind the trees.

*

He had a dream or memory. She was driving a horse between the shafts of a cart or caravan. The horse was brown and white, a circus horse. It clopped along swishing its tail, its eyes were nests of flies. She let the reins fall loose upon the horse's rump. It was marked like the world on a globe, with lands and seas. Its rump was a map of Australia. There was a fly sitting where they had landed, he and she. Look, her finger said, that is where we are going, that is where we will live. And as she spoke they both whirled up in the air and hovered above it all, looking down. Look Markie, her voice said, there is the coast, the coast of Australia. They had been in nowhere for days: up there in the darkness whirling about. He had slept, woken, felt sick, drunk a glass of fizzy water. There had been her hand on his, anchoring him. The journey would never end. She had said, we will soon be there, but he had known better. He had known they were nowhere, lost in space so that soon being there or anywhere had no meaning. He had forgotten everything. Then her finger pointed and there was a crust of white against the blue; even though they were still up here, stranded, unreal.

The horse was real. But the horse was a horse in a story. Somebody had told him that it would be brown and white and go between the shafts of a cart or caravan, going somewhere down a narrow road. But in the story he, Markie, was there too. It was he who took the reins, slapped the fat rump, shook the slow horse on into a trot. He, not his mother. So she was still not there, he could still not find her. Unless of course she was behind him all the time; but he could not turn his head.

On the telephone in the next room Louis was saying things. He heard.

– Buggered off, weeks ago. Left me with the kid.

Markie came close but invisible behind the door, to listen. Louis kicked the door shut. It had no handles. Markie just heard his voice, weary and flat. He pushed and pushed against the door and it flew open. Louis stood with his back to the door, his back to Markie, in trousers and with bare feet. His hair was light with dust and his bare brown shoulders were dusty too.

Markie thought – Everything's got so dirty.

He looked down at his own small square dirty feet – they were both allowed to go barefoot in the house – and remembered that she had washed and dried them once, toe by toe. Not here. Somewhere else, in a bathroom, one that did not have a wood floor and spiders and no towel. He – or someone – sat on her knee while she dried between his toes. There was the hot red bar in front of them. But it was not here, it was gone. He brushed it out of his mind. Louis' feet were filthy too, with black nails. His trousers sagged from a broad belt. His hair was a black bush flecked with dust. The sky beyond him through the window was purple with heat. The trees looked tired today, like Louis. Had anybody ever washed and dried between Louis' toes? Markie went and lay down on the settee, turned his face to the warm smelly plastic and felt tears grow in him like something huge to spit. He felt like the dog, more like the dog today than like Louis, the dog when she had been hit.

Louis came into the room where Markie lay face down and the flies buzzed louder than ever and the black toast crumbs lay on the table in among the old newspapers and bills and the dog sighed.

– Markie, looks like your mother's shot through. You and me'll have to make the best of it. There's fuck-all else I can do. It's no good blubbering. If we all lay down and blubbered where'd we be?

He sat down on the other end of the settee. There was a dead weight about him as if they were on a seesaw; he outweighed Markie so that suddenly Markie shot up into the air on his account. He rose, airborne. Louis was crying. The shock was intoxicating. Nothing so strange had ever happened before. He bobbed up astonished, his own tears dried. He heard his own voice sounding squeaky.

– I don't care. I don't care if she never comes back again.

Louis raised his head. He spoke as if tearing something out of himself. His voice sounded rusty and old.

– Fuck it, Markie, he said, of course you do.

That was when he knew finally; but afterwards he forgot. It was easier to forget things. You could just move on and have tomorrow instead. There was no way of knowing after this how much time passed. She did not come back. It got colder and wetter. Markie knew that he was growing because his clothes no longer fitted and he hardly ever peed the bed, and his turds went neatly into the plastic potty and then he carried them and flushed them away in the dunny. He slept all night and woke when Louis did. He began to be able to dig the hard earth as Louis did, to crack it open and turn it over. Together the two of them went to plant the little green vines that came in plastic bags one day with their woody parts sticking out like liquorice root. They planted them in straight rows in the emptied earth, in the place that his mother had not been able to imagine. They looked small and a bit limp and stick-like when they were planted, but Louis said that they would do.

There was a place on the step where she used to sit, to read or smoke or look into the distance. Without explaining anything to himself Markie took to sitting there. He would cross his legs as she used to and stare into the distance. Straight ahead of him was the wall, the valley full of gum trees, and beyond there was the streak of river. Beyond the river somewhere was the sea. At a particular time of evening it was a good idea to sit here and look out. He brushed the flies from his nose and settled himself on the warm edge of the verandah, sheltered by the rock wall Louis had built. There was an old broken chair just behind him in which the dog lay, her head upon her paws and her open eyes also looking out. It was a good place to sit, a good time to sit here. He watched the sun begin to go down earlier and earlier and earlier and the cold of the evening begin.

Louis said – It's too cold to sit out there now. Come inside.

But what he could not say to Louis was that it was at this time exactly that the bush was full of others. He felt them coming up closer, knew them around him. The dog, who never spoke or said, must feel them too. She might be among them, he was almost sure she was. The sun sank to a certain level and the scrub all around the house became alive with them. The tall whispering gums that were almost like people themselves kept them only just out of sight.

He had no words for them himself. The few words he used these days were entirely for practical solid things, they were objects of barter, nothing else. There was no need with these others, for words. They whispered to him in another language. Or perhaps they were babies, younger even than he was, and had no words themselves only knew what they meant. He sat until the first star came out and his legs and hands were numb with cold. If he had had a cigarette he would have sat and smoked it. It was what men did, he had seen them; they sat out on their verandahs at sunset and smoked a cigarette. Louis called him again from inside the house. The dog, her chair no longer warm from the sun, got up slowly and crept inside, looking back at him over her shoulder. Markie rubbed his cold legs with his cold hands. Every evening he had to sit here, it was his spot. When everything was grey and the night sounds began, after the extraordinary moment of silence when the sun went down, he could go in.

Louis waited for him with cooked vegetables and a bowl of soup. The stove crackled, there was the smell of smoke. They would sit side by side and Louis would drink a beer and they would switch on television and watch something until they nearly feel asleep. The television went on and on, rolling useless words over their heads, showing them useless pictures. Markie would doze and loll against Louis' shoulder. Louis would not say anything for hours on end. Sometimes the silences were so long between them that Markie would forget how to speak and his voice when he used it would come out sounding cracked and strange. Only the television spoke, yakking away about stuff that had no meaning. And outside, between the trees, in the darkness out of sight, there were all the whispers and shuffles and creakings of animals; and the others, retreating into dream.

THE WALL
Helen Lamb

Gourlay positioned himself centre-frame in the kitchen doorway where he could not be missed – the arms folded across
his chest adding bulk to his already hefty presence. He
gazed down the length of the garden to the girl behind the
fence. Her head bobbed down, then reemerged as she let
go another stone and it clattered to the ground, breaking into
the silence of the surrounding gardens, drawing attention to
itself.

Gourlay waited to be noticed. His chin jutted forward a
fraction of an inch. An indifferent half-smile on his lips. Not
too much. He didn't want to seem too friendly. So he settled
on the kind of expression that could be taken one way or
another. The girl was looking over in his general direction but
he wasn't sure if she'd spotted him yet. She seemed to glance
round about him. At the azalea bush in the foreground. At a
window above his head. Then her pale, little eyes glazed over
and slid diagonally down and across the wall, continued
smoothly right over him in the doorway and stopped at the
clump of pampas grass on his right. Her lips twisted up to one
side and she frowned at the pampas as though it particularly
offended her.

So she was ignoring him, Gourlay thought. It made no
difference to him. He had a right to be there and she was
nothing much to look at although she seemed to think she
was. She thought a lot of herself. He could tell by the way her
hands went up to her hair when she thought he was looking.
And, all the time, kidding on she didn't know he was there.
Gourlay decided to call her bluff. Thrusting his hands into his
pockets, he set off deliberately down the garden path. Not too
fast. He didn't want to look like he was going out of his way.

163

The girl came up behind the fence again. She couldn't pretend she didn't see him now.

She looked over briefly, then turned and took off across the garden. The back door slammed. A moment later, Gourlay saw her through the kitchen window.

He stamped back into the house. 'That's an ignorant little bitch,' he said.

His wife looked up from the ironing. 'What's she been saying to you then?' He shrugged. His wife put the iron down to rest. 'She must have said something.'

Gourlay flushed and turned his back on her. He wasn't going to tell her that the girl had ignored him altogether. It made him look stupid. He sat down at the table and flicked through the newspaper until she got the message. He wasn't going to talk about it.

He thought about the girl and the way she'd let the stone crack onto the ground. She could have laid it down. Laid it down nice and quiet without creating a disturbance but that wasn't the way she did it. It was a small detail, maybe, but it seemed to sum her up. She just couldn't make up her mind. First she bends over to lay it down. Then halfway there she lets it go.

She took the same half-hearted line with the boy – bawling him out one minute and laughing the next. She was always laughing with him. If not laughing then smiling. When she smiled her eyes had a funny way of creasing up and disappearing. She never smiled at Gourlay or his wife. Never spoke unless they spoke first. But with the boy her eyes creased up and disappeared as though she had been blinded by love.

The boy didn't look like her at all. For a start, he had black hair and she was a blonde. Not the kind of blonde you get out of a bottle either – more of a mousey blonde. So maybe the boy was like his father – whoever he was. Gourlay didn't know. She probably couldn't make up her mind about that either. A couple of guys were round at her place regularly.

He could hear her outside again. When he got up to look she was tearing down the fence, attacking it with everything she had – hands, feet and various implements – stamping and hammering it into the ground. It left the garden behind her exposed. Gourlay looked out in dismay at the churned up patch of grass, the piles of purple-brown stone and the house, in the background, with its vacant, staring windows.

The stare summed up everything he disliked about her. The poverty she brought with her. The bare bedroom window and the naked bulb in the kitchenette which shone clear across his garden at night – a constant reminder of her presence and her total disregard for the cost of electricity. Her complete lack of everything – material or otherwise. The lack of curtains. The lack of apology. The way she always appeared at the door to call in the boy before he could speak to him. And the way she looked at him through those pale, disinterested, little eyes as though she couldn't be bothered – as though his opinion didn't count.

She just carried on trundling the pram back and forth, adding bit by bit to the pile – two or three slabs of stone at a time and as the pile began to grow Gourlay's paranoia mounted.

He had only pointed out the fence belonged to her so that she would know. It was only right she should know what was hers, her responsibilities and so forth. The posts were on his side which meant maintenance was up to her. That was the general rule with fences and it was fair enough, after all, because she got the better side facing her way. But maybe that's what had got her started.

She must have thought he was complaining about the condition of the fence because it wasn't long after that the stones began to appear. It was small amounts at first. Every day, she pushed the pram up to the field and came back down with a couple of slabs. But, gradually, she began to step up her activities and the loads got heavier. She was making five or six trips, sometimes double, until the wall began to take over – not just her life but Gourlay's as well. He had counted every load as if it was missiles she was stockpiling behind the fence.

When he went out again the girl was digging up a line of turf on the boundary between the two gardens. It was heavy, slow-going work. After a while, she straightened up and said hello. Gourlay didn't return her greeting. He looked right past her at the piles of stone instead. 'You're not going to make much of a job in this weather,' he said.

'Why's that then?'

'Subsidence,' he said flatly. Her wall was going to sink. He looked at her square on and smirked. 'The soil's too damp.'

'You think so?' the girl said. She dug her heel into the earth and stared intently at the ground. Then she leaned over and brought her weight down on the spade.

'Now take that wall over there,' Gourlay said, jerking his thumb towards a low wall behind him. 'That was done right. She wanted a raised bed for her alpines,' he explained. 'Not much to look at if you ask me. I prefer roses myself but it's what she likes.' The girl didn't look too interested in his wall. She stabbed into the ground and jarred the spade against a buried stone.

Gourlay raised his face up to the sky. 'Aye,' he said with some satisfaction. 'It looks like rain.' The girl glanced up balefully and a single drop of rain spat in her eye. Gourlay's lips twitched. The elements were on his side.

The two of them locked in a wordless tussle. The girl flung the spade aside and began to stamp down the earth – short, violent stamps which seemed less directed at the ground than at him. Gourlay folded his arms and watched while he waited for rain and vindication. He knew about things she didn't begin to understand. The weather, for instance. How to build a wall. How to wait. Something that simple.

Gourlay knew how to wait. He'd made a career out of waiting – twenty-five years as a traffic warden. And, over that time, he'd perfected the art of standing about, minimising the amount of exertion necessary to maintain the upright position. He didn't slouch or stand too straight or shift his weight from one foot to another. He didn't even tighten his jaw.

When he stood he just relaxed into it and became completely immobile except for his eyes which flickered occasionally over the girl. She was on the skinny side. Hair pulled straight back from her face and a shapeless black sweater that came down almost to her knees. She had freckled skin and small pale green eyes which creased up whenever she spoke. So she would look or speak but not both together. Not that she did much of either. She ignored him most of the time.

Gourlay had come across some stuck up bitches in his professional capacity. He always gave the snooty ones a ticket. But some of the others. You would be surprised. Some fine-looking women park on double yellow lines. He smiled to himself and looked at the girl side on.

'The woman before you,' he said. He paused for a moment to remind himself of the voluptuous widow in her early forties who had been the previous tenant. The woman before her had been something to look at. Big. Plump. Blooming. Gourlay's taste in women had a lot in common with his taste in flowers. He liked them a bit showy.

'She wasn't interested in the garden,' Gourlay said. 'She wasn't lazy though. Always working. Busy busy. Couldn't stop. I think it was some kind of compulsion but it was decorating with her.' Gourlay frowned and looked thoughtful for a second. 'I think it has something to do with that house,' he said. 'It seems to make people restless.' The girl raised her eyebrows and carried on stamping. Gourlay cocked his head to one side. 'What are you doing that for?' he inquired.

She didn't answer. She slapped the first stone down between them. 'You could be doing with a hand,' Gourlay said.

She slapped down another stone. 'Are you offering?'

'Tsk. I wasn't meaning myself.' Gourlay was genuinely surprised. He'd been thinking more about one of the men he sometimes saw round at her place. 'Maybe one of your fellas would give a hand if you asked nicely,' he said.

The girl looked up sharply. 'Maybe I don't want to ask anyone nicely.' She had the missile ready in her hand – a small wedge-shaped lump of stone. She took a step back and weighed it up in both hands for a moment as though she couldn't decide what to do with it. In the end, she let it drop. She bent forward, tugged at the hem of her sweater and began to peel it slowly up over her head. He caught a glimpse of white midriff and soft pink under-garment riding up over angular ribs. The girl let the sweater fall where she stood and tucked the pink vest into the waist-band of her jeans. The colour seemed to warm and soften her. Her eyes glowed. Her pale skin took on a subtle lustre. But Gourlay barely noticed any of this. He was transfixed by the outline of small hard breasts beneath the flimsy stretched material.

He thrust his hands deeper into his pockets. The girl was watching him. She'd hardly given him a straight look since she moved in. Her eyes always strayed off to one side or glanced right by him. But now she was looking right at him – her pale little eyes wide with contempt. 'Looks like you were wrong about the rain,' she said.

Gourlay didn't answer. He sucked up the saliva behind his teeth and allowed his gaze to return to her breasts before taking aim. *Not much there to look at.* He spat directly onto the stone she had just laid, then turned back to the house.

In the kitchen, he pulled down the blind. The bitch was kidding herself if she thought he had any interest in her whatsoever. She was nothing special. Line her up with half a dozen parking violations picked at random off the street and he wouldn't give her a second glance. She wouldn't even merit the time it took to write out a ticket.

He poured himself a cup of tea from the pot his wife had left on the stove and sat down at the table. The tea was black and bitter. He heard the boy come back from school. Their voices murmuring together for a moment. A ripple of laughter from the girl and then a shout. GET DOWN. A short tense silence followed before the boy began to roar and Gourlay's wife came bustling into the kitchen. 'What are you sitting through here in the dark for?' She yanked up the blind to see what all the noise was about. 'Would you look at that,' she said.

The boy was lying flat on his back, flailing his arms and legs and yelling fit to bust. The girl was laughing. She grabbed him by the ankles and began to work his legs back and forth like pistons. The boy yelled louder. 'I know what I would do with him,' his wife said.

'Sure you do,' Gourlay replied. He got up and left the room.

Gourlay spent the rest of the evening slumped in front of

the television set. His wife appeared at regular intervals with mugs of tea and updates on the girl's progress with the wall. She was still out there at the back of nine. At ten o'clock, his wife popped her head round the door again to say that she was off to bed and that the girl had gone in for the night.

Gourlay sat on in the gathering gloom listening to the creaking overhead as his wife prepared for bed. And long after she settled he was still sitting there – absolutely motionless. His mind motionless also – except for one slow, growing thought. The girl had humiliated him. He wasn't exactly sure how she'd done it but he knew all the same. He knew. Even in the dark, with nobody to observe him, his heart raced and he flushed at the thought. He got up and went through to the kitchen.

Her light was still on. It illuminated the length of her garden and the bottom corner of his own. The low, ragged outline of the wall ranged between them. It wasn't done yet. She would be out again tomorrow.

The girl came into the kitchen and stopped directly below the light. Her face was white and intense. He could see her through the window very clearly. The pink vest. The black sweater slung across her shoulder. She'd let down her hair and it seemed to float about her head in a pale almost transparent cloud. She stood there for a long time, staring out at the wall, apparently unaware that he was watching.

Then, suddenly, her gaze shifted to Gourlay's darkened window. Her lips twisted to one side and her eyes appeared to fix on him. Gourlay ducked as though he'd been caught in the glare of a searchlight and banged his elbow on the table. When he came up again he saw the girl smiling – a secret, satisfied smile – as she turned and walked out of view. The wall was there between them now and that was what she wanted.

QUIET, IN THIS TIME OF CHANGE
Esther Woolfson

From his memory of years, he held one episode carefully in his mind from an ordinary afternoon during his last school holiday. It was just lighting the lamps, nothing else. There had been no significance to the day, nothing to make the weightless, easy splash of paraffin, the sharp, dry smell of matchwood special. It was one of those moments when, for no reason he knew, time slowed and stilled, altered everything, then moved on.

He had watched himself resolve that late afternoon out of a brown haze of semi-darkness, hover at first above the lamp, grow as the light grew into narrow, angular shoulders and thin chest, till he was whole, tall for fifteen, peculiarly pale, luminous, almost sinister, underlit by new, bright, sulphur light. In the shadowed mirror he watched a whiskered white ghost moth flitter a circuit nearer and nearer the hissing radiance of the lamp till, unwilling to witness its death, he turned, reached out and collected it in his two closed hands. Its wing beats were like a failing heart inside his palms – his own heart quickened nervily to its pace and he knew he would find grey, smoky streaks from it on his skin after it was gone. He opened the mesh door and released it, aware that while he did, another dozen were flying in and in the course of that dark evening would blaze themselves fatally into the beautiful ambit of his light.

Another term had gone by since the moment of time slowing. It had disappeared into a web of afternoons, history, prayers, casual brutality and expedient friendships. It was a difficult time, they all said, this time before change. The newspapers said it, the chaplain when he rose to address morning assembly urged them to patience, to acceptance, to open their hearts in this difficult time. The sound of the choir practising carols in the chapel beyond the cricket field filtered through grey, hot early mornings. The rainy season was beginning, the long holidays soon, then Christmas.

'Open your hearts!'

His heart felt closed. There were things you had to keep closed if you wanted to protect them.

'Keep the pen moving! D'you hear? Keep it moving!'

His pen, which had not stopped moving, trailed its pattern across the jotter cover, a spider's thread of lines creeping over onto the white paper of his homework. The shout stopped short of him, addressed to a broad-backed boy with skin the burnt red of brick idling at the desk in front of him. He had watched the red boy taking time from his work to lift heavy arms briefly above his head.

'You! Stupid! Write something!'

The strange, singular, afternoon philosophy. During prep, you must write. Anything. Your name, the word God again and again on the pages of your notebook, concealed so that the gs and ds formed the tangents of an indecipherable, never to be unravelled rope of lines and curlicues – blasphemy, to write the name of God several times purposelessly in succession, even in anguish. If pressed, you could copy the nursery rhymes stuck on the walls of the classroom where during the day, big, backward boys from every small corner of the country sat, being taught things they would never learn now.

Whenever he passed their classroom and looked into the open wedge of doorway, he felt disquiet, embarrassment, which died away into embers of sadness. It was all over for them, he thought, quickly, finally, entirely without point. Some of them, though, he hated. They had even stopped looking like boys and had already become men, solid as he was still not solid, hairy with pillar legs bulging from uniform shorts, shaved faces, wide, thick-skulled heads.

When he had come into the room early in the afternoon, two stapled sheets of paper lay on each desk. He knew it was the rota for patrol duty and though he did not look for his name, he was aware it would appear on it this time. Avoiding letting his eye fall upon any names, he put it quickly into the back of his history book. He could not expunge from his thoughts the only words which flashed to his look, words printed in heavy type at the top of the rota, 'You will meet at the groundsman's hut at seven p.m.'

Looking around the hot, still room, he saw the endless movement of hands on pens dragging ink into trails, letters, words, sequential lines, fathomless equations. His pattern grew and formed a wayward, flowing frame to his history homework. By now, he could move his hand to form the pattern without looking at it while his gaze flicked over the heads, across the room, through the window to the sky rolling grey and purple clouds over the horizon. Still moving his hand, he looked back to the page.

'By 1896, the peoples of the south . . .'

During his three years at the school, he had waited to get used to it. Everyone said he would but he never did. Slowly, he began to accept that life has no forward movement outside time, no inexorable progress towards hope.

A time of change. Change took people in different ways. Here, it was quiet change, steady and inevitable and not like the terrible, incandescent blow-outs which had happened in other countries.

All the same, there were already gaps in the room, chairs empty. Most of the ones who had left had people who had come originally from South Africa and had now gone back. Some of them he did not miss – bullies, boys who boasted their energetic catalogues of cruelty and petty viciousness. They had not all been like that. Nor had all the bullies gone. The boys whose families were staying were people with nowhere else to go, people who had been born in the country, as he had been, or felt something for the place; missionaries or doctors, refugees, poor lay preachers, farmers whose land would never buy them a farm further south. He thought of Andrzej's family's mean, unyielding land of stones and knew that they could never leave. He knew that some boys' parents were considering going but were prepared, at least, to wait and see.

'These are difficult times,' the headmaster said. He said it with careful, nervous relish, not every morning but two or three times a week after prayers, as a sermon or a warning or a way to explain the meaninglessness of the day.

Three years. Newness waned, passed, turned slowly into unbearable familiarity. Still he felt he moved in a small, tight circle from one point of strangeness to another, the unreality of the new becoming the unreality of experience.

'Where're you from? You're not from here.'

He told them he was, that his father was too. He told them the province where they lived, the village, the nearest town, as if the sound of familiar names might act as a talisman in their appeasement.

'Where're your folks from?'

'Originally? Scotland. Missionaries.'

They clustered round his bed, where he was unpacking his things, tall, short-haired, like eager animals.

'What's your old man do?'

'A doctor.'

They thought it was funny, and began calling him 'doc', shouting it from the other end of the long, shady dormitory. 'Ey, doc! Many whites up your way?'

Someone asked how old he was, then why he was so small. Why so thin. So pale. Like a girl, someone else had said, like a girl. Pretty. Girlie.

Brant, Valhoen, Davidson, Koosman.

'Like a girl. Isn't he? Girlie.'

When, three months before, he had announced that they were to begin night patrols, the headmaster's soft, pale, puffy face had been flushed, spotted bright with the responsibility. He talked to the boys of what was appropriate during a State of Emergency, about the vigilance of man and of God.

*

For the few months before he was sent to school, after he knew
when he was to go, he worried among other things, about the
lighting of the lamps. He had never missed a day except when
he and his father travelled away from home which they did
every few months for the duration of his father's rural clinics,
three or four days at most. They never went away for holidays.
It was his habit to wander, grubbing deep in silent limestone
caves, hollow warrens of shaft-lit emptiness, searching among
the scrub and thorn trees of the flood plain to the west of his
home, stalking wild cats – small, fleet, sharp-toothed genets,
gold-eyed civets whose dun, banded fur he coveted, vervet
monkeys, chameleons, rock hyraxes. He went watchless,
making himself read the time from the air, from the slant of
sun on the soft ochre rock, from the small, late movement of
beasts towards water. Running or freewheeling his old Raleigh
bike over fissured rock paths and invisible bush tracks,
through head-high palisades of grasses and dry, stunted trees,
he could gain time, gathering momentum on steep rock falls,
eroded sand banks carrying him yards for no effort, and arrive
back at the top of the hill just as the air of dusk was thickening
with insects and the slow twilight fall of dust.

He remembered an afternoon, walking on the ridge with his
father, early, before the sun was gone, the soft 'hoo, hoo' of
wood-pigeons resonant in the air.
　'I wish you didn't have to go away to school.'
　'What choice is there?'
　'I could leave here, move to town.'
　'No!' He could and would imagine no other life and if his
going ensured its continuation, his not being there to live it in
the way he had, was, he realised for the first time, a part of a
pact he had entered.

His life had been secure even after his mother had died. He
hardly remembered her. He was not certain he knew why she
had died. He had been small and remembered a confusion of
unexplained events, waking in the night, being taken to sleep
in a strange bed, happenings which had meant he was sud-

denly alone and then with only his father. Singing hymns in church when he was small, he had waited to see if his mother might come in through the low door in a sudden explosion of sunshine. When he was old enough to winnow thoughts into separate, discrete strands he understood why he had thought that and why it had never happened. By then, it was already too late to ask his father anything more. The church was low and warm, its darkness split by rods of sunlight which parted the dust through gaps in the roof. Sermons were long, soporific and dull, but he liked the easy, reverent come and go of village people, patients still in pyjamas, small children, dogs in patches of sunlight. The dogs were only thrown out when their fighting interrupted the sermon.

He raised his eyes from his homework and looked out of the open window to check the changes in the sky. He was waiting earnestly for rain, for the hot tedium of the dry months to end, to be dashed apart by the force of clouds bursting, the first thunderous fall of new rain. He would run outside to feel it begin, slow, promising drips overtaken suddenly by a wide, white, sweeping curtain which would wash over him in the brilliant, drenching spate which would bring a new life to his body as it would an explosion of life from the anhydrous earth. Last year, he had stood in the first rain with Andrzej. They had watched the clouds for days and were out waiting as soon as the first dark, madder splashes stained the gravel path. As it began, the drops were big, warm, slow, splashing with the warmth and spatter of blood until it came faster, colder, flying chill from their shoulders, coursing in thick, clear, twisting eddies like transparent, external veins down their arms and over the backs of their hands, falling in narrow, glistening waterfalls from their fingers. He had watched Andrzej tip his head to the dark sky, swallowing the water running between his lips, rain gathering, glittering, in the deep corners of his tight-closed eyes. The long seaweed filaments of Andrzej's hair had floated and swayed in the lucent fall of water down his thin, brown neck.

It would be days still, he reckoned, days. He hunched

forward, stretching one cramped leg at a time under the desk. He had grown tall in the three years.

He had always been good with lamps, getting them lit first time without wasting paraffin, building up quick, regular pressure, trimming off wicks, changing mantles, even when he was small. It was his task for the doing whenever he was at home. His father had let him light the lamps from the time he could reach up to the table, long before most parents would have allowed a small child to touch matches and jerry-cans of paraffin. Because his mother was dead, he was allowed to do these things. In all his years of lighting, he had never broken a lamp or knocked one over, set fire to the house or to himself as people round about often did. He had seen them lying, mute, wide-eyed under the hospital's white sheets, his father saying quietly at the open doorway, 'House fire.'

Lightning struck people's fragile houses of corrugated iron, breeze block and board and his father spent nights with people beyond saving.

Lightning was common during the country's volatile rains.

Their house, his and his father's, had a tile roof and solid walls, inside plumbing, a verandah and smooth, polished floors. In the rainy season, lightning cracked from the tiles and dispersed back into the electric air.

The hospital had a small generator which often went wrong, but when it worked, it made the low building glow across the night like a ship on an ocean. Its light created an outer, darker darkness. One day, the hospital, the village, the small settlement to the south, would be hooked up onto the country's electricity grid, but till then darkness, unbroken except by pinpoints of fire, prevailed. Even by the striking of a match, he felt part of time itself, bisecting the night with fire. In spite of the paraffin and fine, friable mantles, he knew it still to be fire. Outside in the late, dark moonless bush, nothing broke the blackness but, seen from a rise, small disparate flares of amber flowered from the fitful streamers of white smoke which rose every evening just before dusk. He had learned to adjust his lighting times to the change of weather and season.

At school, there was electricity. Dormitories and dining halls oscillated under the chain-hung blue of fluorescents which hummed and flickered and lit with dead but livid light. Every week, the staff of house servants climbed up with ladders and cloths to scrape gummy black films of insect mess from the tubes.

'What's this?'

'A photograph. What d'you think it is?'

He had hidden it carefully. He looked at it only on the rare moments when he was alone in the dormitory. It vitally increased the acuteness of his misery. There were moments when he needed it to be acute, moments when it was easier to bear than the dull, common thud of everyday unhappiness. They raked casually through people's things as if innocently, searching their books, their clothes, picking at things as small children might, commenting, asking questions, making public.

'A photograph?'

The photograph was of his primary school. He remembered the day it had been taken, the bright morning when his father lined them up outside the schoolhouse, the tallest smiling at the back, the gap-toothed infants cross-legged at the front, himself smiling in the middle row. Mr Mwenga was in the centre back, a whole head shorter than the tallest children. He too was smiling.

'Jesus Christ. Look at this!'

'He was at a kaffir school!'

At first, they had laughed.

'Christ, man, you're kidding!'

'Let me see! Jee-zuz! Hey look, look at this man, hey look at this!'

'Christ Almighty!'

'A kaffir boetie? Eh?'

'Jesus Christ!'

The words he heard when they woke him up that night. Kaffir boetie.

*

'It's something which will happen,' his father said to him when he was small and asked what independence was, 'and so it should. It will happen in time and nobody will stop it.'

He had always thought himself lucky, to go to school every day. Some of his friends went every day, many less often. Most had work to do guarding herds of stick-boned cows, scattering wood-ash on vegetable patches, carrying enamel bowls of groundnuts to the small, weekly market, preparing boxes of charcoal for sale. He went to school morning and afternoon. After school they played with washed-out tin cans he had taken from the dustbin at home, filling them in the muddy water of the furrow, made twig bicycles which they puttered in their hands along the grey dust tracks, cars from the emptied husks of monkey oranges. They roamed the bush looking for trees of wild fruit, white globes of masafwa, the dry paste of the mpundu which was always too high to reach. They shared the fallen fruit, each sucking the tiny sliver which, however sweet it seemed, pulled in their cheeks and dried their mouths to a grimace.

In those days, when his father came back from the hospital in the late afternoons, they took out the books sent by the correspondence school in London and learned sums and handwriting and grammar together until supper.

Mr Mwenga shouted but rarely at him. From Mr Mwenga he learned some more sums and to sing hymns properly in harmony like the other children did and ever after he could entertain a dormitory with Mr Mwenga's rendition of the Lord's Prayer.

'Ey, fellows, listen to this. He's got this old boy's voice to a T. Go on, say it,' and he would stand on the wavery, moving springs of his bed and recite to hoots and applause.

'Our Father who art in heaven, hallowed be thy name . . .'

He enjoyed it when they laughed but afterwards he always lay wakeful and uneasy in the dark.

Often in the past year or so when he was at home he saw people come up the long sand road, three or four in a car, black as well as white, almost always men. They went first to the hospital and his father would ask them to the house for tea. Later, his father would say to him,

'More special pleading.'

During the last holidays, a group had arrived late one afternoon, after the lamps were lit. They had come straight to the house looking for his father. He watched them outside on the step, tall white men in a uniform he did not recognise. They were not police or game wardens but wore an unfamiliar insignia on their khaki uniform shirts. Listening from his room, he heard the sound of raised voices, his father say,

'Never! You want to drag us into your own morass!'

The men left shortly after, calling back out of the dark, their words without bodies suddenly devoid of meaning, calling hopelessly from the night.

'We'll remember,' one shouted, 'we'll take a note of that, doc., mission station or not.'

'Dangerous maniacs,' his father said to him, leaning against the door frame, bemused. 'Men who can't grasp the concept of the lost cause. I'd be concerned if I thought they had any real support.'

Quiet, in this time of change.

Sometimes at school, he found a newspaper abandoned on the table in the common room. When he did, he took it to the lavatory to read. Occasionally he told his father in his letters about an editorial he had read or about an election rally he had passed on his way to town at the weekend, but mostly, he wrote about school work, complained about calculus and physics, re-told some old Latin pun. His father's letters were detailed, technical accounts of operations, the management of an unusual snake bite, the progress of inevitable sepsis after wounds inflicted by crocodiles.

'What's your old man going to vote, girlie? What would you vote?'

*

179

When he was at home, they listened to the wireless news every evening. He found it difficult to reconcile the remote, scornful tone of World Service broadcasts about the country with being there, his own reality diminishing theirs to nothing. The reports reduced them to a few words from the mouth of some-one called the Commonwealth Secretary. An unwanted, tire-some problem, another planet, a different dimension in time.

'Bloody fools,' his father hissed, listening to the broadcasts. 'Bloody fools.'

There was a wireless at school but it was a way to conjure a nightmare, to imagine yourself walking up to the small group who lolled in their chairs round it listening to light music from South Africa, saying, 'Can we listen to the news?'

'Hey, the boy who said he'd vote independence. What d'you know!'

A time of change. A difficult time. They all said so, the headmaster, the chaplain, the radio.

Nightly, through the dark evenings and into the silent hours of morning, three boys patrolled the wire-lined perimeter of the school, halting their hourly circuits where the school drive met the quiet, almost traffic-less road. The wire ended there by the drive in stout metal uprights near a cluster of frangipani trees and grass down at the end of the drive where sixth form boys sat on Sunday afternoons with the girls from the girls' school down the road who brought them gifts of biscuits they had baked in domestic science lessons. The girls were not allowed in further than the frangipanis. There never had been gates.

Although the school was in the suburbs of the city, he was hardly aware of the city's existence. During the week, it was as if the school was lost in the wilderness of some ever-altering bush, surrounded by landscapes which in his mind changed minute by minute as he manipulated topography, saw in low cloud, foothill and mountain, endless grass veld beyond the dazzle of noon light. Every day of term-time, he could pinpoint a moment while it was almost day, late afternoon balancing on the thin, still edge of sunset, before night swallowed up the red remains of sun; black, opaque and total night. He could never forget where he was, the school noises a crude, pervasive hum wrought from raised voices, the seismic clanging of kitchen pots, slamming doors reverberating infinitely through his body and head, even in the tiled lavatory stalls where still there was no peace.

'Another ten minutes. If you aren't finishing your work by now, you're in dead trouble, hear, dead trouble.'

Jackson, the day's prep supervisor, had the demeanour of the policeman he had once been; ill-tempered, suspicious, he was short and neckless, his bristled pink hog's skin sprouting white, coarse hairs on the back of his head where it folded into his shoulders. Jan Valhoen said that Jackson had been converted to God by a prisoner. Valhoen was a policeman's son, reckoned by some to know.

'He saw Jesus appear, like that, in the cell. Thought at first it was his sergeant. Honest. I'm telling you. My old man told me. It's got to be true.'

Other people had other stories. Whatever, Jackson was no longer a policeman but sat frowning, round and glistening, marking jotters, stopping from time to time to wipe away the ink which his hot, tight fingers melted from the pages.

He had met Andrzej on the first evening he arrived at the school. Andrzej had come quietly into the dim dormitory and stood in the arc of light thrown by the half-moon window. He was carrying an old case made from thready, greenish canvas, a soft, white bag squared off by its contents of books over his shoulder. Andrzej looked, to his eyes at least, strange, thin and tall and dark, made of something different from other people, his skin smoother, the yellow brown of old ivory, his joints appearing uniquely aligned, allowing him movement proscribed to other people by cartilage and bone and tendon, his arms lifting lightly, his hands bending, folding, fingers spreading on the bone like the wings of birds.

'Have you just come?' Andrzej bent to put his things down

on a bed. His dark hair was so long as to fall across his face
as he did.

'Yes.'

Andrzej offered his hand.

'Andrzej.'

'Have you just come too?'

'Me? Today yes. But I'm already two years here. I'm a
Pole. Dark, dago Pole.'

He had noticed the timbre of Andrzej's laugh, high and
mirthless.

'The first day's very bad,' he said. 'You feel like hell.'

'I suppose so.'

'On the journey,' he said, 'I always cry.'

'How much should you do? How much were you given? Then
do the five, goat-head.' Jackson raised his eyes momentarily
from his marking, impatience hovering edgily in his voice.
They always said that people's tempers became fragile in the
short time before the rain began.

He had never actually cried on the journey. He had wanted
to. He thought often about the first journey. Margaret, a nurs-
ing sister from New Zealand who had worked at the hospital
for a few years, had brought him. His father could never get
away for long enough.

'I don't mind taking him,' she said, 'it'll be good. I'll get to
see the school. Have some time in town.'

The journey made him feel a strange bond with her, a staring,
blue-eyed woman whose strong body looked as if it was banded
with iron under her flowered frocks, an uncomfortable intimacy
in spite of his long-standing antipathy towards her. She had
always expected of him some unknown code of New Zealand
suburb manners. He was amused by her perpetual impatience
with the country, with the lack of electricity, the absence of comfort, the dearth of shops. As she drove, she swore under her
breath, chaste New Zealand curses which he enjoyed hearing,
real ones adapted for Christian use, near enough genuine to
carry some force but just outside the wilderness of sacrilege.

They had put up for a night in the house of a minister friend of Margaret's in a small town halfway between home and the school. The house had brown lawns and a wooden balcony with a broken rail. Throughout the house, notices were pinned giving incontrovertible instructions: Clean the Bath, Leave the Soap in the Soap Dish, Close the Shutters Before You Switch The Light On, Trust In God. They had tried to be nice to him but he was deeply in the the throes of his own taciturnity. He remembered it very well every time he made the journey, bumping miles of dull, hot emptiness.

'We're not in the best of moods,' he had heard Margaret say through the house's thin partition walls.

Six hundred miles, give or take.

He had sat looking out at the dry, hot towns, miles of scrub and rock. The cloud of powerlessness he felt enveloped him, obscuring his view of a future. He could recreate the nauseating emptiness of it still when he passed through a particular town. Mechanically, he could calculate how many miles till they were there and he would again feel the surge of anxiety and sore, gouging hollowness every time they passed that place with its one flowering bougainvillaea, its three broken-down cars and its row of Indian stores.

'Everyone here goes away to school,' Margaret had said at intervals. 'Cheer up.'

His father had stood on the road and watched them go.

He heard stories about the school long before he came. They were not unusual stories, just the ones told about schools, about initiation ceremonies, humiliations, petty slavery.

'Bastards at that place. It's a fact. The things I could tell you . . .' John Rankin, the son of a visiting missionary from the west had been pleased to set light to the small bush fires of anxiety he already felt. They had sat one afternoon shortly before he had been due to begin at the school, the verandah step warm under their legs, watching evening crows flock in quarrelsome, gritty clouds like free-floating black flakes of bonfire soot to the tops of the blue gum trees in front of the house. Their fathers, friends from childhood, were drinking tea inside. John Rankin was home for the holidays from his boarding school in Scotland.

'What things?'

'Better not say. Wouldn't be fair.'

'Tell me.'

'Just things. You know how it is. People say things.'

'Like what?'

'Just about the kind of people who go, what they do, you know the sort of thing.'

'Of course. But what else've you heard? You might as well tell me.'

'Well that's all, honest.'

'It's run by missionaries.'

John Rankin had laughed, throwing back his head, showing the jerky movement of a stringy, white Adam's apple.

'My God,' he had said, 'they're the worst.'

His first sight of the school's low, red roofs, broad verandahs, white walls, wide, gleaming windows had reassured him — surely this was a place of civility, of order and pleasantness. A late, deep-rose afternoon light made the wide, busy streets of the city, scattered houses, jacaranda and hibiscus trees look curiously mild, attractive and unreal. He and Margaret lifted his trunk from the car boot on to the fine pink gravel.

'Oh come on,' she said in her flat, admit-of-no-feeling New Zealand voice, 'nothing's ever that bad.'

She drove off towards the centre of the city.

He let his chameleon go before he left. He thought about how it had been for a moment reluctant, hovering sluggishly on his hand, seeming not to want to part from him but then had stepped with its careful toes on to the branch and within a second was gone among the glint and dapple of green and yellow cassia.

'Kaffir boetie! Jesus Christ!'

*

Recalling John Rankin's stories much later, he found their force was spent. They had never really frightened him. They had been romantic, stagey diversions. He wished they had been real.

His friendship with Andrzej had seemed easy, propitious. He thought about it a great deal after Andrzej's death. It was Andrzej who had known how to make friendship easy, Andrzej who offered glimpses of a world beyond the fall of fluorescent light, a world which till then, he had never known existed. He had responded too to Andrzej's mordant, sombre moods which had made him feel helpful, made him believe he understood the existence of a state which outreached simple misery. Although he was only a couple of years older, Andrzej often seemed like an adult bestowing favours. On weekends when he was in luck, Andrzej walked into town with him, strolled about the city streets, sharing a bottle of fizzy drink on the way back to school, both of them too poor to afford their own.

Andrzej's family were five years in the country, and farmed a smallholding in the east.

'Poor land for farming. Nothing grows. Rock grows, beautiful rock. Thorns too, like forests. Scorpions like jewels. That's what we grow. Fine crop, eh?'

Without Andrzej, the place was viler, emptier, its possibilities ever bleaker but otherwise, it was unchanged. He found people to sit with at meals or who were going into town or occasionally to the cinema on Saturdays and he would join a group of them, but following Andrzej's death, he felt he had no friends.

'OK, end of time. Put your things away. Stand up for prayers.'

They stood, scraping their chairs back, leaning the backs of their hot, damp knees gratefully against the seat edges, swaying, shaking down their hands, their numbing feet. It was a surprise when Jackson stood. He was not much taller than when he was sitting and now his wide, damp shorts were creased and stained into waistband and crotch.

'Heads down. Jesus our father, help us to be more like you.

Teach us the way to live as you lived, in goodness, truth and mercy. Amen.'

'Amen,' they said and began to break from their momentary stillness.

'OK. Git.'

The room began to clear.

He picked up his books.

'You.'

He turned.

Koosman was taller than he was, broad, dense and fair. His eyes were small, his cheeks too big. From a distance, he had a crazy look as if the wrong bits had been used in assembling him, tiny hands, protuberant pigeon's chest, strange, long straight-calfed legs. His skin was fair and peeled off in white dry flakes. His lips looked as if they would crack open and bleed if he stretched them to smile.

'Ey, did you hear?'

He raised his eyebrows to invite Koosman to speak, breathing in the stale, warm air through his nose.

'Did you hear? I need to hear you heard. No mistakes, eh?'

'What, Koosman?' he said.

'Good, glad you heard. Aren't you going to look? See who you're on patrol with?'

'I'll look at it later.'

'You'll look at it now.'

He shrugged and took out the piece of paper.

'OK, I'll look at it now. It's not a big deal. I don't know why you get so excited.'

'Sure it's not a big deal. Just look and see who you're with. Going to be good fun, eh?' He put his hands up, two fists in front of his face in a configuration of shooting.

'Vrrrrrrr!'

'For God's sake, Koosman!'

'Seven at the groundsman's hut, girlie.'

Walking from the classroom, he read down the list. There was no order to the arrangement that he could discern. The headmaster, Mackenzie, chose and wrote the names. He knew very well who had been responsible for Andrzej's death.

Dusk was a short, short time. You had to hurry before dark. Floodlights were switched on at six to illuminate the grounds. It was important to see who walked across the school's territory. It was important to know if anyone crossed the watered green lawns or the carefully kept pitches, to rout out of his hiding place anyone who would wilfully conceal himself in the tiled corridors, the glassed-in walkways, the pavilion, the silent, empty chapel.

The groundsman's hut was at the far end of the pitch, a place heavy with the fume of creosote and charcoal, the full, nauseating smell of the groundsman's meals of maize and twigs of noisome dried fish. Next to the shelves of plant pots and twine, roses for watering cans, stakes and stumps and wickets, the junk of groundsmen and gardeners, the carpenter had put up hooks for clubs and an open hanging rack of small pigeon holes to contain torches and whistles.

He whiled the time till seven. It was too hot to be inside, too hot to be outdoors. He walked in the heavy dusk to the chapel but did not go in. He never went in these days unless he had to for assembly or on Sundays and even then he held himself away from the drab, hieratic procedures. Sitting on the grass outside, he listened to the choir's practice, the soar and ebb playing over him, painful, thrilling but strangely alien. He watched the lights come on behind the tall modern windows.

In the eight months since Andrzej's death, he had learned to avoid them. He knew the rhythm of their footfalls, the pattern of their breathing, how their shadows fell against walls. He could recognise in near darkness the cast and bob of their walks, the tilt of their heads, their elbows, how they held their hands and feet. There was no practical purpose to his keenness of eye. He still had to sleep in the same dormitory but he felt he preserved some area of his own by moving swiftly away from their pews in church, away from the tables where they sat over their food.

*

'Wait till after independence, when everyone comes here. Then they'll learn all kinds of new lessons, our friends. All kinds of new lessons.' Maybe Andrzej had been right.

Since the beginning of that term, he had felt uneasy. When he had seen Andrzej on the first day back, he knew he had been frightened for him.

'The Pole's back!'

'Hey you're the wrong colour for here. Someone's made a mistake.'

They nagged at Andrzej like a dog shaking a stick, tossing and worrying a bone, never quite ripping into the bluish strings of membrane, never quite shattering the bone's white surface.

'Cut your hair, pansy!'

'Christ, it's the greasy Pole.'

Then for some reason, he had thought there was a fine bubble, a shell of distance, of urbanity, transparent but strong, around Andrzej. He had forgotten to be vigilant.

'See your friend? Well, I'm telling you, he's a dirty shit!'

'Leave him alone, bastards!'

They copied his voice, making it too high, imitating the intonation, second generation, Scottish intonation, like his father's, not quite like theirs, like a song or a hymn or an incantation, but too high.

'Leave him alone, bastards!'

'Bastard? Who's a bastard?'

Brant's elbow had held him down against the bed, into the choking folds of the pillow.

'Go on then, do something.'

Andrzej's screaming was like the screaming you could hear in the bush any night, noise struck from darkness and silence when everything for a moment stopped and then, horribly, the tremulous, quick voice of something caught, screaming its high, final scream.

'Dirty shit, your friend.' Brant pushed him further into the mattress. 'Dirty shit. Deserves what he's getting.'

*

The longest night, that night or the subsequent nights, he never knew, nights when throughout the darkened room, breathing sounded, faltered, went quiet, when the crickets' sudden hush was louder than their constant buzz, buzz, buzz. No one moved, spoke, slept, lifted up their heads, even when the day sounds started, the odd car on the road, servants clanging and singing in the kitchens in the first moments of the stealthy orange dawn.

'What's happened?' he had whispered in the morning when the room had emptied. He pulled the blankets from Andrzej's head. Razor-skimmed patches shone from his scalp while strands of long hair still hung from circles of pale skin. Andrzej lay, his face in the pillow.

'I'll go and tell someone, I'll go to Mackenzie now.'

In his office, Mackenzie had been choosing hymns for assembly. He had listened, suggested that he should speak to them all later in the day.

'When tempers have cooled,' he had said, 'when tempers have cooled. Now come on, let's have a smile. I don't like long faces at assembly.' At assembly that morning, they sang 'Guide Me Oh Thou Great Jehovah' and 'Angels From the Realms of Glory'.

Later, entering the dormitory which for once was bright, he noticed first a brilliant blur, a dazzle of intense whiteness, Andrzej's forehead like glass, brighter, whiter even than the light, then, peeling back the sticking, wet, grey blanket, tugging at the sheet's drying adhesions, he had felt the cold prickle slowly up his body, slowly, realising, slowly, holding the blanket, peeling it back, slowly, feeling as if he was, in spite of himself, opening another black wound.

'Jesus, he's killed himself!'
'You're kidding!'

Afterwards, they said that it had only been a joke, that he was nuts, they hadn't known it would upset him.

*

'I think he was killed.'

The policeman had been surprised.

'There's no evidence of it.'

'You don't have to hold the knife in your hand, do you?' he had said, hopelessly.

'Oh, but you do,' the policeman said, looking at him with pale, glassy eyes, 'oh, but you do.'

Mackenzie allowed him to go to the funeral. A student teacher out from Ireland for six months was sent too, to represent the school.

'Just to show our sympathy,' the headmaster said, raising his eyes, staring at nothing, forgetful, distant, 'a gesture.'

'Terrible thing,' Patrick Dritten said, frowning, glancing into the mirror. He drove timorously between the high walls of copper lorries which pulled out to pass, fast, without warning. 'A boy of his age.'

Patrick Dritten's slow, carefully casual voice rose on an expectant, questioning tone. He realised that Dritten would forever associate the country in his mind with death, that later, back home in Ireland, he would find the sun, banks of rain clouds, dry sand paths, tied together in his memory with the unremitting, solitary rope of death.

He told Patrick Dritten what he knew of the towns they passed, the names of trees, how long it would be before the next filling station.

Andrzej's parents' farm was on high land, on the edge of the escarpment.

'There's been trouble for the place. You know, the place.'

He had walked with Andrzej's father a little way from the house to look out over the edge of land into the deep, wooded, purple cleft which split the surface of the earth. Mr Wyciecz spoke hesitantly, uneasy, beginning tears.

'The place?' He realised that Mr Wyciecz's English did not have the right words for the situation.

'The ground, the ground. You know. The priest says, the ground. The priest.'

The man's voice urged him to understand.

'The ground,' he said, quietly, making scooping movements with his brown fingers.

Andrzej's grave was made on the dry edge of the graveyard beyond the shade of a triangle of forlorn thorn trees. There were no defined boundaries to the graveyard and he wondered how the priest made the difference between one patch of dust and stones and another. The land fell sharply behind them down into the valley. He had thought about asking if he could bring a plant to grow on the raised, raw mound which was the grave, but he knew he would never again pass this bleak road end. In any case, for the first few days Mrs Wyciecz would carry a pan of water down to pour around it and after a few days more she would forget and come only once, twice a week. By then it would have begun to shrivel and she would no longer want to water it. A jasmine or a rose or a bright Cape Gooseberry.

The Wycieczs' had no indoor plumbing. Their house was a divided shed, sitting room, kitchen, a couple of curtained-off bedrooms. The lavatory was a shack down a path behind the house, a simple pit latrine scraped down over the dark blue cleft of the escarpment, facing the hazed, empty void.

After the funeral meal, he excused himself from the cabin and found his way to the shack. It was dark by then and very clear, the moon full and so bright he had no need of a torch. The lavatory faced the valley and whoever had built the shack had made a free-swinging half door so that a sitter could, unseen, look out over the changes of hour and season.

The sky seemed distant that night, deep, veiled across with the fine gauze frost of the Milky Way, the air so thin that that he found breathing difficult, breathing and weeping and looking out into the ineffable, chill, endless darkness before him falling sheer into the void at his feet. He knew he was the last and final thing on the edge of some unknown, desperate world.

*

Seven, at the groundsman's shed. The groundsman was sitting out in front, a charcoal brazier burning. He gave out heavy, metal banded wooden clubs, whistles, torches.

'It quiet, boys. You come back here, get a warm.'

At midnight, the floodlights switched off. The air was suddenly deep, black, warm, like warm, dark water.

About them, the city began to go quiet, the noise of night creatures overtaking the city's sounds, crickets louder than engine racket, frogs beginning their low, bass chorus, stopping, croaking on.

'Bleddy frogs!'

'I like to hear them.'

They threw their clubs on the ground and leaned against the springy wire of the fence.

'They stop me hearing if there's anyone about.'

'Anyone about? There hasn't been a car for an hour. The last person we saw on the road was at nine.'

'Look, you don't know. You don't ever know.'

'For God's sake, what do you expect? An insurrection? What would they be doing here? At this place?' He laughed.

'Don't laugh,' Koosman's voice was unsteady, 'don't you laugh. They take over key installations, right?'

'Who do? Anyway, this isn't a key installation. This is a pathetic white boarding-school that's no use to anyone.' He began to hum.

'Jesus, shut up!'

Clouds blew across the moon. It was still hot at midnight.

They heard the man before they saw him. They heard the faint, rhythmic squeak, a noise so faint that it might have been the air whistling down their noses, coming again, again, like breathing.

He was wheeling a bicycle along the path to the chapel, black against grey like a crow flying at dusk.

'Hey man, come on!'

The torchlight in the man's eyes stopped him but he looked into the darkness beyond it, unafraid.

'Evening, sir,' he said into the darkness, 'evening.' He was elderly, his hair greying round his high forehead.

'What are you doing here?' Koosman stood over him.

'Going home from work, sir, the Hotel Nile, you know the Hotel Nile? I clear the bar, close up, go home.'

Koosman's whistle sounded oddly muffled, though it brought Valhoen warily round the corner of the chapel.

'Hey, who's he?'

'That's what we're asking. What d'you want here? Why're you here, eh?'

'Short way home, sir.'

Valhoen grabbed the handlebars of the man's bicycle. In the strong beam of torchlight, it was plainly a cheap Chinese bicycle, the kind no boy at the school wanted to admit to owning, the kind people made jokes about, about how they fell to pieces on bumps on the road, about how they were the counterpoint of the Chinese matches whose sulphurous heads flew off and set light to your clothes except they were not like the matches, not things which fell to bits on the the road, they were what men like this one used to cross a silent, night-time city. The man struggled after it, held away by Koosman's broad arm.

'Look, leave him alone. He's just going home. Leave him.'

'Christ, 'e's got no business here.' Valhoen pushed the man's shoulder. 'No business, hear? Who are you with?'

'With? Just me, sir, sorry. I'll go on. Give me the bike, I'll be off.'

'No, oh no, you can't just come in here when you like, see, you might be anyone.' Valhoen threw the bike against the ground and began to kick it.

'How do I know why you're here? Eh?'

'Are you after something? Who else is with you? Someone else eh?' Koosman was shouting now.

'No,' the man said. 'No.' A reasonable voice. 'No, sir. Going home, that's all, sir.'

It was hearing the man say 'sir' which made him stop, breathe in and shriek, 'Don't call him "sir"!'

The man looked from one to the other.

'Don't call that scum "sir", d'you hear?'

The frame of the bike had buckled, the front wheels standing at right-angles to the bending crossbar, oddly angled, the wheels like two twisted, worried faces.

'Stop that!'

'What?'

'Christ, I told you, Valhoen, stop that.'

Valhoen's foot lifted.

'Valhoen.' His voice rose, unfamiliar, loud. 'Valhoen!'

The club lay on the path. He bent for it and as Valhoen's foot fell again, he measured the inches, felt the lead-heavy swing of the wood, back, saw before he swung, the weight's own, perfect, dynamic curve.

'Don't!' he heard Koosman yell. 'Christ, don't.'

It was as if he heard the club smash full under Valhoen's broad nose, as if he felt the quick silent snap of bone, the easy slide of it up, up into tissue and blood.

'Please! Don't!'

The club swung down and dropped heavy against his knee and he threw it back down onto the dry black grass. He turned from where Valhoen was hunched, bent, his head covered by his arms, from Koosman, from the man now beginning to stand the bike on the distorted, grimacing Os of the wheels. The man's head, he noticed, now shook, fear or the infirmity of age causing it to shake, lightly, back and forth in a thin, disseminating tremor.

He turned to walk back over the grass and raised his head to look at the moon, pale, hazed behind a flaking curtain of cloud, then suddenly clear and silver against the sky as the cloud blew and passed. When the rain began everything would have that odd, wet smell. He tried to think of what it was, that smell, but could think only of water and iron, salt perhaps, and earth.

Biographical Notes

ALISON ARMSTRONG was born in 1964 and, after studying in London, moved to Alloa in 1989. Her non-writing occupations have included that of childcare worker, journalist, teacher and night-club manager.

ROSALIND BRACKENBURY was born in 1942 and brought up in the south of England. She moved to Scotland in 1982 and now lives in Edinburgh. She has published eight novels and two collections of poems and is currently working on a novel. She has recently spent time travelling in Australia and in Morocco.

ELIZABETH BURNS lives in Edinburgh. 'The Smallholding' is her third story to be published in this annual collection and her poetry has been published in the collection *Ophelia and other Poems* (Polygon, 1991).

SUSAN CHANEY was born in Cambridge in 1951 and now lives in Edinburgh with her three children. Her short stories have been published in several anthologies, including *New Writing Scotland*, *Original Prints* and *Scottish Short Stories*. She received a Scottish Arts Council bursary in 1989 and has recently completed her first novel, *The House Within*.

ROBERT DODDS was born in 1955. He read English at Oxford and has worked as a teacher and lecturer in England, Mexico and the USA. He is married with two children and now lives in Edinburgh, where he is Lecturer in Film and Video Production at Edinburgh College of Art. A number of his short stories have been broadcast on BBC Radio.

G. W. FRASER was born in Burghead, Moray and educated at Elgin Academy, Aberdeen University and the University of Leicester, where he now lectures in physics. He is married with two children. A member of Leicester Writers' Club, 'Pen' is his second published short story.

DONNEIL KENNEDY has lived in London, Isle of Tiree, Lagos (Nigeria) and Glasgow. His varied occupations have included that of chartered surveyor, singer, actor and restaurateur. He was awarded the prize for best radio play in the STV/Radio Clyde comedy writers competition and was runner-up in the *Macallan/Scotland on Sunday* short story competition. One of only five twentieth-century writers included in the *Everyman Book of British Ballads*, he is currently working on two novels.

KEVIN LAING grew up and went to school in Fife, and later studied English Language and Literature at Edinburgh University. He is currently living in Denmark, where he works as an English teacher and continues to practise creative writing.

HELEN LAMB lives in Dunblane. Her work has previously appeared in various anthologies and magazines and on radio.

G. M. MCFADDEN believes writing helped to cure his childhood stammer. He has lived in Glasgow since the age of eighteen, although he was brought up in the north-east of Scotland. Now in his forties, he devotes much more time to writing, concentrating on short fiction.

GEORGINA MCINTOSH was born in Falkirk in 1965. She has had stories published in *Chapman* and *West Coast* magazines. She is a winner of the Young Scottish Playwrights Award. 'I eat my peas with honey' is also published in *The Edinburgh Review* 1992.

LORN MACINTYRE was born in Argyll. He is a full-time writer, and writes *The Thinker* column for the *Glasgow Herald*. Two of the three novels in his *Chronicles of Invernevis* series, *Cruel in the Shadow* and *The Blind Bend*, have been published by HarperCollins.

DONALD MUNRO was born in 1962 of a Glasgow Highland family. He has worked as a freelance writer since 1990, writing plays, poetry and short stories in Gaelic and English in addition to archaeological and historical journalism. He is married with one son and lives in a forest on the shores of Loch Etive.

GILLIAN NELSON was born in Kent but educated mainly in Edinburgh and has lived near Inverness since 1980. Of her four published novels, two (*The Cypress Room* and *A Secret Life*) are set in the Highlands. Her non-fiction includes *Highland Bridges*, a history of northern Scottish bridges. She is married to a mathematician and has three children.

WILLIE ORR was born in Northern Ireland in 1940, leaving the province in 1959 to work as hill shepherd in the Western Highlands of Scotland until 1974. He attended Stirling and Strathclyde universities as a mature student and now lives in Argyll, writing and teaching. 'The Butterfly' is his fourth story to appear in this annual collection.

JANET PAISLEY lives in Falkirk. She is a full-time writer and her short stories have appeared in *Original Prints* 4 and *New Writing Scotland* 8 and 9. Her poetry collections include *Images* (Moray House), *Pegasus in Flight* and *Biting through Skins* (Rookbook). She was Writing Fellow for Glasgow District Libraries (South Division) 1991–1992.

FRANK SHON was born and educated in Arbroath. He has had a varied life punctuated by a spell in the army, a degree at Bishop Otter College, Sussex and extensive travels in Australia and India. He now lives in Athens.

IAIN CRICHTON SMITH was born in 1928 on the island of Lewis. He writes novels, short stories, poetry, plays and criticism, both in English and Gaelic. His novel *An Honourable Death* (Macmillan) and a collection of poetry *Collected Poems* (Carcanet) will be published this year.

ALAN SPENCE was born in Glasgow in 1947. His published work includes a short story collection, *Its Colours They are Fine*, two books of poetry, *Ah!* and *Glasgow Zen*, and three plays, *Sailmaker*, *Space Invaders* and *Changed Days*. His novel, *The Magic Flute*, won the 1991 People's Prize. He is currently Writer-in-Residence at Edinburgh University and he and his wife run the Sri Chinmoy Meditation Centre in Edinburgh.

ESTHER WOOLFSON was born in Glasgow and educated at the Hebrew University of Jerusalem and Edinburgh University. She now lives in Aberdeen. 'Quiet, in This Time of Change' is her third story to be published in this annual collection.